YOU CAN DRAW

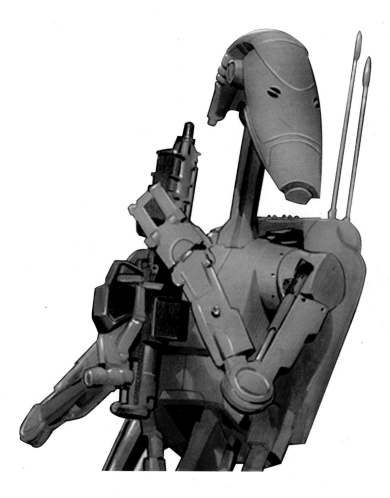

LONDON, NEW YORK, MUNICH,
MELBOURNE, AND DELHI

DK PUBLISHING

PROJECT EDITOR Heather Scott   PUBLISHING MANAGER Simon Beecroft
SENIOR ART EDITOR Nick Avery   CATEGORY PUBLISHER Alex Allan
SENIOR DESIGNER/BRAND MANAGER Lisa Lanzarini   PRODUCTION Rochelle Talary
DTP DESIGNER Hanna Ländin

LUCASFILM

EXECUTIVE EDITOR Jonathan W. Rinzler
ART DIRECTOR Troy Alders
CONTINUITY SUPERVISOR Leland Chee

SD242—10/06
First published in the United States in 2007
by DK Publishing
375 Hudson Street
New York, New York 10014

10 11 10 9 8 7

A catalog record is available from the Library of Congress for this book

ISBN 978-0-7566-2343-2

Hi-res workflow proofed by Wyndeham Icon Limited, UK
Design & digital artworking by Nick Avery
Printed and bound in China by Leo Paper Group

Discover more at
www.dk.com
www.starwars.com

YOU CAN DRAW

STAR WARS

BY BONNIE BURTON
ILLUSTRATED BY MATT BUSCH AND TOM HODGES

CONTENTS

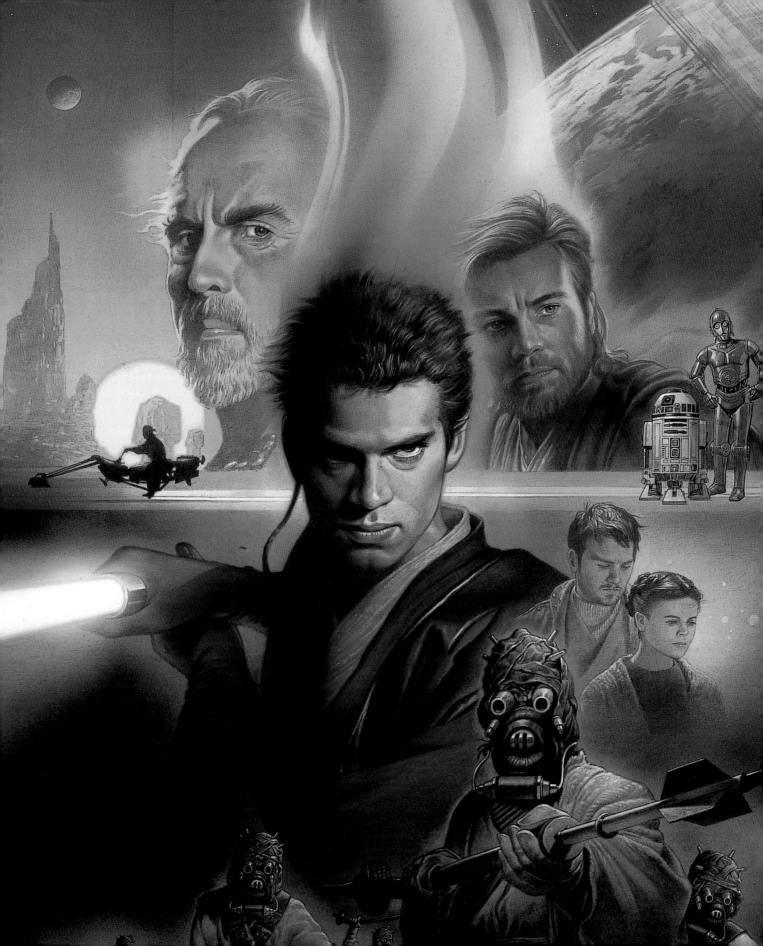

INTRODUCTION

Ever wanted to draw *Star Wars* characters just like the professional comic-book artists but don't know where to start? This book gives you the techniques to draw everyone from the loyal R2-D2 to the charming rogue Han Solo.

You'll learn all kinds of cool and useful techniques that artists use to bring their sketches to life. However, before you can transform any stick figure into a Sith figure, you need to remember one thing—practice!

Draw all the time. Whether it's on a napkin as you eat breakfast, in the margins of a magazine when you're riding the bus, or on a piece of scrap paper when chatting on the phone. The more you practice these techniques, the better artist you'll become.

One more thing—this book won't turn you into an expert overnight. Just as these skills take practice to master, you need patience to do them right. If you don't have patience then you'll end up a frustrated mess—like Anakin Skywalker. And you know what happened to him!

So practice, be patient, and above all—have fun!

PENCIL DRAWING

With a mere pencil—and a little imagination—drawing characters from a galaxy far, far away is easier than you think! All characters start as stick figures made from lines and basic shapes. Even General Grievous began life on the page as just a few innocent lines and triangles. Once you understand how to sketch figures, adding dimension with shading will be easy!

In the next few chapters, you'll also learn about body anatomy so you'll be able to transform your stick figures into flesh-and-blood *Star Wars* characters. Check out the handy tips on artist tools and tricks of the trade like shading, foreshortening, and perspective.

The basics are all here, complete with plenty of illustrated examples and step-by-step tutorials to get you started. Before you know it, you'll have a sketchbook full of droids, Jedi, Sith, aliens, starships, and space battles!

EQUIPMENT

PENCILS

Just as each Jedi Master has a favorite lightsaber, every artist has a preferred pencil type. A standard pencil has many grades to choose from, while a mechanical pencil holds thin strips of refillable graphite. To make a mark that doesn't show on photocopies, artists also use blue pencils.

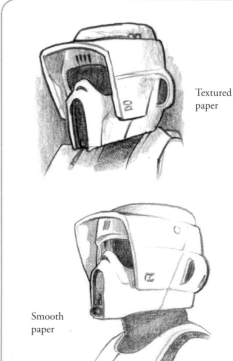

Textured paper

Smooth paper

Pencil sharpener

Mechanical pencil

Graphite refills for mechanical pencil

Wood-clinched graphite pencils

Wood-clinched graphite pencil with eraser

Blue pencil

Paper

Some artists like smooth paper because the pencil glides across the page with ease, while other artists love the way their pencils drag against textured paper. Try drawing the same character in notebooks, fancy sketchbooks, or even on the side of a brown paper bag to achieve many kinds of effects.

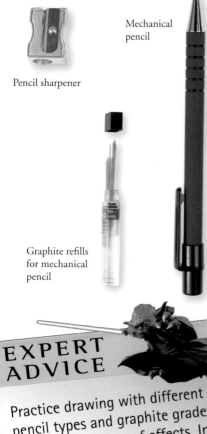

EXPERT ADVICE

Practice drawing with different pencil types and graphite grades to obtain a variety of effects. In addition to these, try drawing with colored, charcoal, sepia, and old pencils found at the bottom of your desk drawer. Each kind of pencil gives a unique look to a sketch. One pencil that may be unsuitable for one type of drawing might be perfect for another. Don't be afraid to experiment—that's how you learn!

PENCIL GRIP

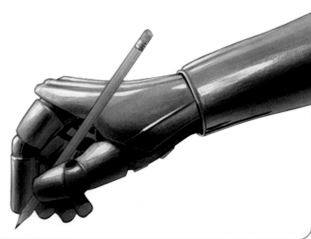

Artists sketch fast and light. So hold your pencil firmly —but not too tightly— between your thumb and index finger. Be aware of the amount of pressure you put on your pencil—too much and you may damage the paper or the pencil. And most importantly—relax your hand and wrist! The goal is to create consistent lines and to have fun!

PENCIL MARKS

Drawing pencils are available in varying grades. "H" stands for "hard" while "B" is for "blackness." Pencils 4H and above are harder graphite, while 4B and above are increasingly softer graphite. If you want a medium pencil, use HB.

6H **4H** **2H** **HB** **2B** **6B**

Erasers

Kneaded eraser

Basic eraser

Eraser pen

White vinyl eraser

We all learn from our mistakes (except for Anakin), so don't worry about ruining your potential masterpiece. Drawing like a pro takes plenty of practice. Keep the lines you like and erase the ones you don't. A basic rubber eraser works, but leaves a trail of tiny pieces. Both kneaded and white vinyl erasers are crumble-proof, and an eraser pen is perfect for precise fixes.

Other equipment

Rulers offer a nice straight edge, but an artist's toolbox is full of other useful items such as a compass, French curves, triangles, and stencils that create smooth swirls, perfect circles, and all sizes of geometric shapes.

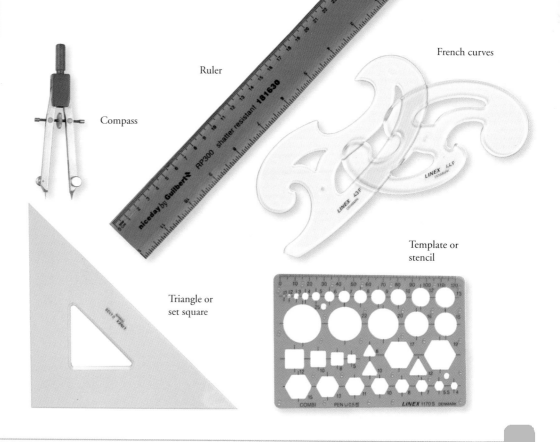

Compass

Ruler

French curves

Triangle or set square

Template or stencil

BASIC SHAPES

SHAPING UP

Every object in the *Star Wars* galaxy is made up of simple shapes. Before you can draw R2-D2 or the *Millennium Falcon* it's important to learn how to draw basic shapes first. Here are three groups of the most useful shapes to help you get started.

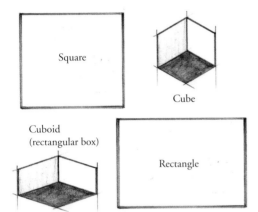

Square

Cube

Cuboid
(rectangular box)

Rectangle

Squares, cubes, rectangles, and cuboids

If you look closely at everyday objects around your house you might spot a few squares, rectangles, and cubes lurking within—whether it's a cereal box, a picture frame, or this very book!

Triangles and pyramids

You don't have to travel to Egypt to find a pyramid. Camping tents, party hats, and ice-cream cones all consist of triangle and pyramid shapes.

Pyramid

Triangle

Circles, spheres, and cylinders

To find two of these shapes, just drink a glass of water! The glass is a cylinder and its base is a circle. Pin-pong balls, baseballs, and bowling balls are all good examples of different sized spheres.

Cylinder

Sphere

Circle

HIDDEN SHAPES

Now that you know the three basic shape groups, see if you can spot them in these *Star Wars* droids, weapons, communication devices, and other items.

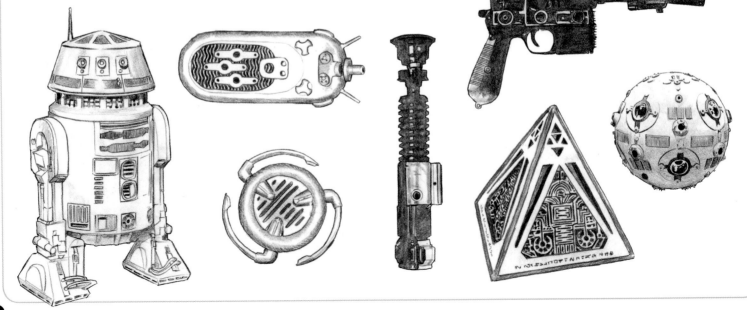

VEHICLES: MILLENNIUM FALCON

"PUNCH IT, CHEWIE!"

The fastest hunk of junk in the galaxy is made up of all three shape groups. The base is made of two ellipses (circles at an angle), and the cockpit is cylindrical in shape. More circles act as engine vents, and the radar dish. The gun turret, shield generators, and various ship panels are made up of rectangles, cubes, and triangles.

Guideline

1) Sketching light lines, draw the base by placing two ellipses on top of each other. Next draw a smaller ellipse on the top, off-center. Add a wedge made from rectangles to indicate the front of the ship. Draw "guide" lines to show you where to put more detailed elements.

Cockpit

Radar dish

2) As you add lines and circles, the ship begins to take shape. Add another ellipse for the gunner's window and more circles to create the radar dish and vents. Give the ship's hull dimension by adding long rectangles with angled sides.

3) This is how your drawing will look once you have mastered all the techniques in this book. It shows how simple shapes can be built up to a complex illustration once you add detail, shading, and perspective.

STEP-BY-STEP

YOUR TURN!

Even though all objects are initially created using simple shapes, getting from the first step to the polished end result isn't always easy. Before tackling the *Millennium Falcon* look at reference photos of the ship in various magazines and books. *Star Wars Incredible Cross-Sections* (published by DK) is a fantastic resource to see the tiniest details on many memorable ships.

THE FIGURE

STICK WITH IT

Just as our bodies are supported by an intricate structure of bones, any *Star Wars* character you draw starts as a series of basic shapes connected by lines. Begin each drawing with a simple stick figure like the one below.

Stick figure

With the head slightly tilted, this figure keeps his attentive gaze directly on his opponent.

The leg lines are at different heights to show that the character is standing at an angle.

This vertical line represents the spine of the figure. If it's curved, your character is bending or twisting.

Drawing the front foot a bit larger than the back foot makes it look closer.

PRACTICE MAKES PERFECT

Not all stick figures are alike. They all have a head, torso, limbs, feet, and hands, but they don't all stand in the same position or have identical proportions. Inject some personality into your stick figure by giving it expressive gestures with unexpected placements for the arms and hands. Activate it using different stances. Draw stick figures of these characters to see if you can identify where the limbs bend, and the angles of the body.

EXPERT ADVICE

It's easier to start from the head downward. Make sure the head is in proportion to the body. Next, sketch the line that will act as the spine. Then lightly draw the other parts of the body. Experiment with a variety of poses. And remember: nothing needs to be perfect at this point!

Follow these steps to draw young Anakin Skywalker. Remember to start by sketching with loose, light lines; add details and darker lines as you progress.

1) Draw a circle for the top part and a rectangle with a wide triangle below for the lower half of his head. Draw a vertical line down the middle and horizontal lines to show where his eyes, nose, and mouth will go.

2) Lightly sketch the lines of his upper torso. Various lines indicate his spine, collarbone and arms; the small circles show the balls and joints of his shoulders, elbows, and hands.

STEP-BY-STEP

6) Finally, add shading. This technique (discussed on page 22) takes a lot of practice so don't worry if it doesn't look like this illustration. Just give it a go!

3) Sketch his lower body; add circles for knees. Make his back leg shorter to show that his body is twisted.

4) Give the figure more shape and muscle tone by fleshing it out.

5) Lightly sketch in the Jedi robe, belt, boots, lightsaber, and finer facial attributes. Erase the lines you initially used as guides. Darken other lines to add contour and depth.

MALE AND FEMALE FIGURE

THE RIGHT PROPORTIONS

Characters come in all shapes and sizes but the key to creating a believable drawing is to keep all the body parts in proportion. This means that the legs, arms, torso, feet, hands, and head should all fit together accurately. Keep in mind that while some characters are short and small (Anakin as a child), other characters can be tall and lanky (Jar Jar).

THE MEASUREMENTS

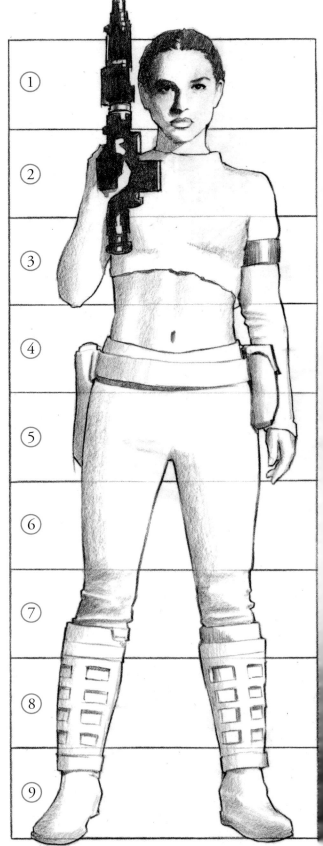

All figures are approximately nine heads high. When drawing a female, however, remember that she will be less muscular and slightly shorter than a male. The female head should be smaller. She'll also have a slender waist and wider hips.

1. Start by drawing a grid nine boxes high with a vertical line down the center (called the vertical axis). The first box will have an oval for the head of the figure.

2. The female's shoulders measure around two heads wide across the body. As you draw, make sure not to add too much bulk.

3. At the breast line, the female form widens to some extent, but will narrow as you draw near the waist.

4. Keep a smooth line throughout the stomach and abdominal area. Add slight bends in the elbow so the figure doesn't appear too stiff.

5. Next sketch the hips wider than the waist. Also keep the wrists narrow.

6. As your pencil works its way down the form, begin to taper off the bottom of the thigh into the leg, and continue narrowing toward the knees.

7. Once you hit the calves, widen the leg slightly to account for muscle tone.

8. Continue to taper the leg as you hit the top of her boot.

9. Remember to add a heel to the boot!

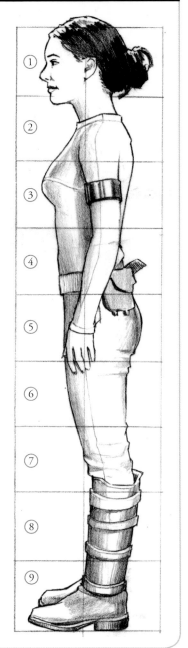

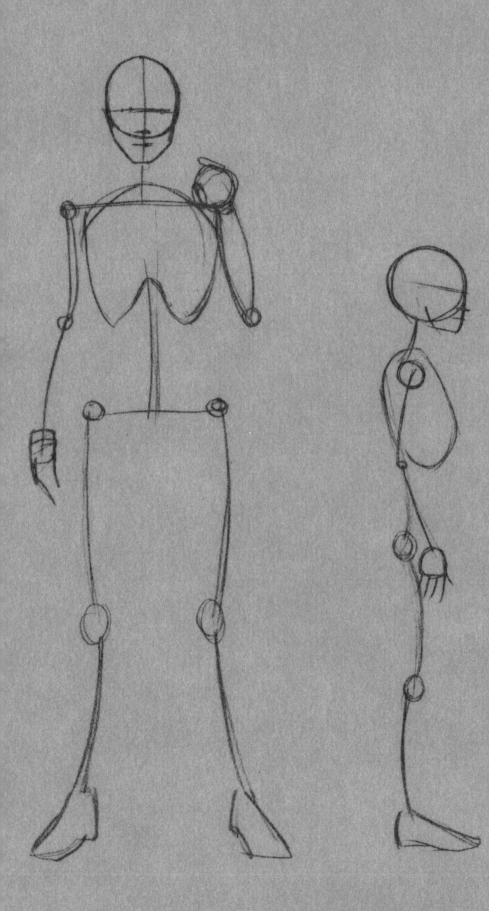

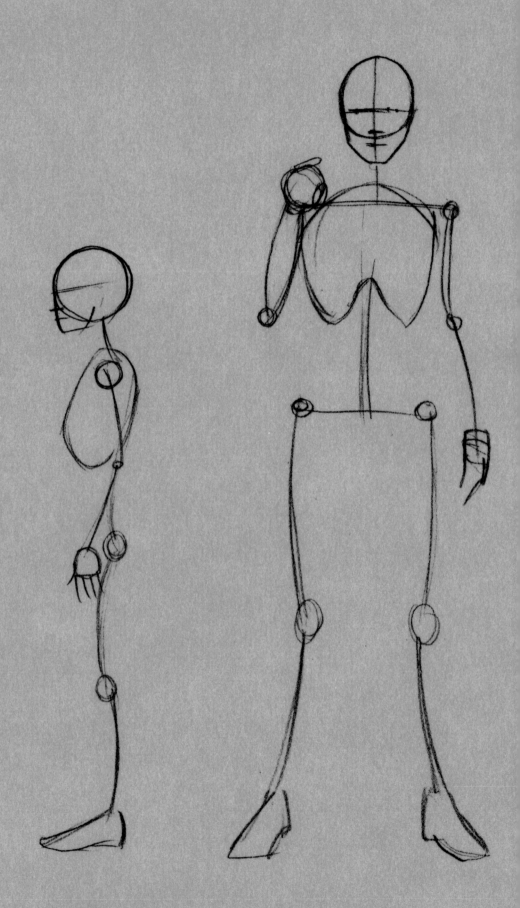

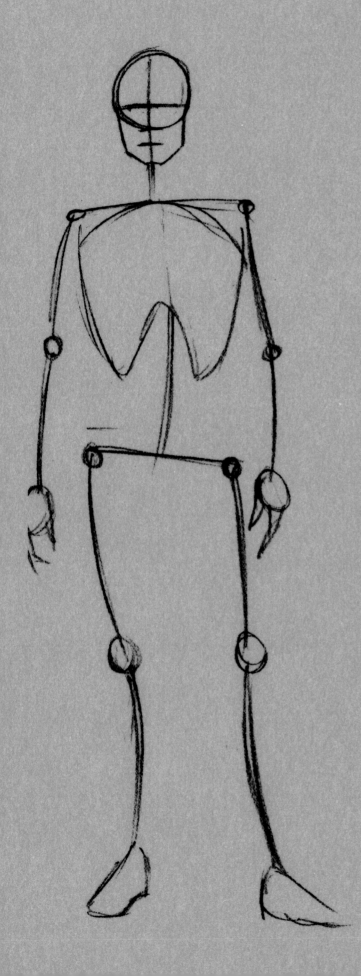
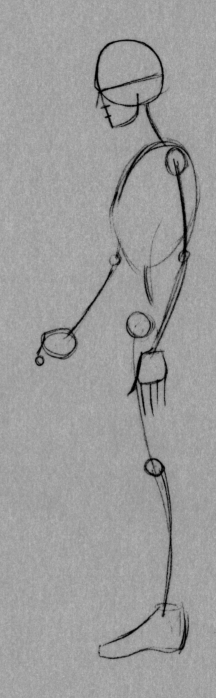

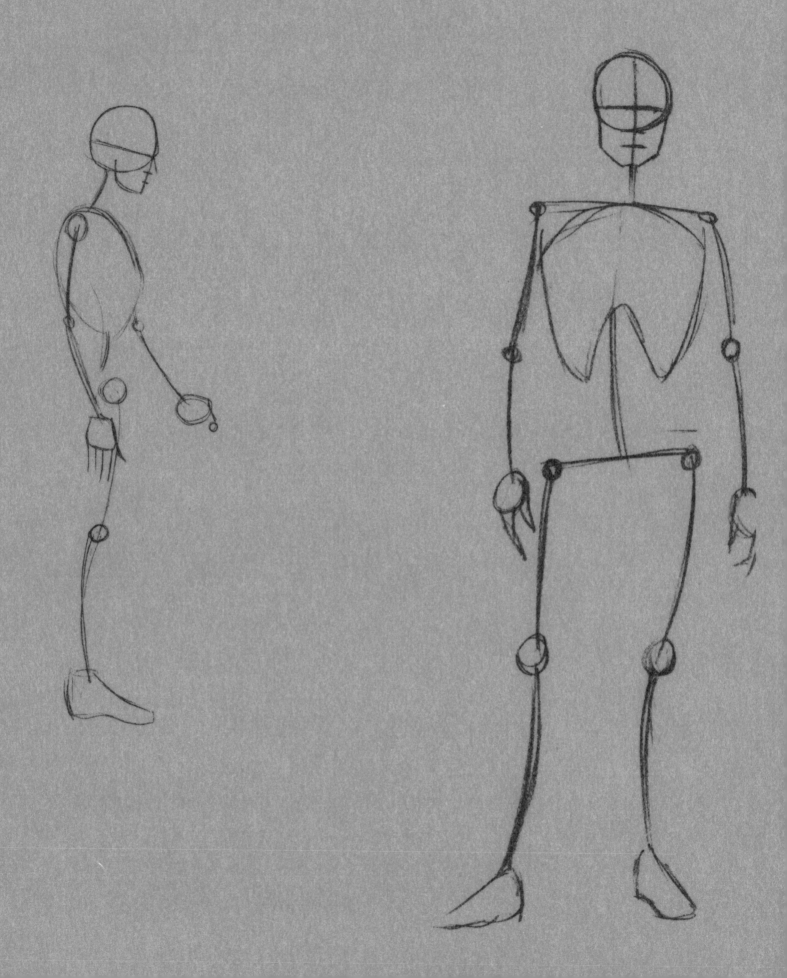

THE MEASUREMENTS

The male figure is also nine heads high. As you draw, take note that he will, in this case, be more muscular and taller than the female.

1. Draw a grid nine boxes high with a vertical axis. Then draw an oval for the head of the figure.

2. Again, the male's shoulders measure around two heads wide across the body. For bulky characters, such as Chewbacca, the shoulders will be three heads wide.

3. Han's arms are fairly standard in size; however, the larger the male figure, the bulkier his biceps.

4. The biceps narrow into forearms. The waistline is also narrower than the chest area.

5. Han's legs slightly widen from the trunk, and his arms are relaxed at his sides.

6. His legs begin to narrow toward the knees.

7. Remember to keep Han's knees somewhat bent, so he doesn't seem too rigid.

8. Continue to taper the leg as you near the feet.

9. The ankles and feet finish Han off at his boots.

Han Solo

The arrogant, yet charming, mercenary pirate Han Solo doesn't need an expansive wardrobe to get the job done. His black vest, light shirt, captain's trousers, action boots, quick-draw holster, and trusty blaster pistol will do just fine.

BATTLE

Even with the Force, the Jedi cannot fight battle droids alone. The clone troopers come to their aid, fighting side by side against the immense droid army. The right use of color, shading, and character placement creates a dynamic Clone Wars battle scene.

MUSCLE!

MAY THE FLEX BE WITH YOU

A character with bulging muscles indicates brute strength and physical power. It also means major damage for any opponent brave—or foolish—enough to step up for a fight. While many characters in the *Star Wars* saga prefer to use elegant weaponry, or the mysterious energy of the Force, to fight their battles, others like to combine talents with their intimidating physique.

YOUR TURN!

Head over to your local library to find illustrated medical guides and anatomy books (e.g., *Gray's Anatomy*). There are also plenty of online sites that show how muscle systems work. Look at detailed illustrations of muscle groups in the arms, torso, and legs in various states of motion to see how muscles look when they are flexing, holding a weapon, or relaxed.

MUSCULAR STRUCTURE

To draw muscles, you need to know a bit about how muscles work. There are several different types of muscles in the body. Some cannot be seen from the outside, such as your heart muscles and the muscles that move the irises in your eyes. The muscles in your arms and legs work in pairs: one stretches (gets longer) while the other contracts (gets shorter). For example, as Darth Maul raises and lowers his forearm, his bicep muscle contracts and his tricep muscle relaxes.

Comic-book artists often exaggerate the arm muscles to make a character look stronger or more threatening!

Bicep

Tricep

BACK STRUCTURE

1. Semispinalis Capitis
2. Deltoid
3. Triceps
4. Latissimus Dorsi
5. Gluteus Maximus
6. Semitendinosus
7. Biceps Femoris
8. Gastrocnemius

FRONT STRUCTURE

1. Frontalis
2. Trapezius
3. Pectoralis Major
4. Deltoid
5. Biceps
6. Brachioradialis
7. External Abdominal Oblique
8. Rectus Femoris
9. Vastus Lateralis
10. Sartorius
11. Peroneus Longus

SHADING & LIGHT

SHADING EFFECT

Above
Light from above creates strong contrast. Use the smooth shading technique.

Behind
Light from behind diffuses the darkness. Smudge with a finger to achieve this effect.

In front
Use smooth shading but leave the top left of the sphere almost completely white.

In front and behind
Shade the bottom and inner edge to make a rim, adding depth.

A SHADING FURTHER

Just as there is a light and dark side of the Force, with every image you draw there should be both white and black tones to give an image depth. Shading with black tones adds dimension to any illustration, making it jump off the page.

Crosshatching
Parallel lines are called hatching. More lines on top and at an angle are called crosshatching. The closer the lines are, the darker the image will be.

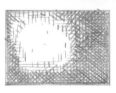

Smooth shading
For a softer-looking appearance, use the side of your pencil to shade in darker areas. Smudge with your finger for a smoother effect.

DRAMATIC LIGHTS: EMPEROR PALPATINE

STEP-BY-STEP

1) Start with basic shapes to draw the head. Draw vertical and horizontal guidelines to indicate where facial features such as his eyes, nose, mouth, and chin will appear.

Guidelines

3) Use both hatching and smooth shading techniques to show where the darkness spreads across the Emperor's face and hood. Shade in other crevices such as his eye sockets and the corners of his sinister smile.

2) As you add his features, make a mental note of where the light will hit his face once you add his hood.

SHADING FACES

The Emperor is indeed a shadowy character, so take your time in shading in every crooked crevice, wicked wrinkle, and tarnished tooth. His face has texture and depth, so as the light shines in front of his creepy gaze, let the contrast of the light and darkness reveal his true emotion.

SERVICE DROIDS

"ARTOO!" "ARE NOT!"

Everyone's favorite astromech droid, R2-D2 is more than just a "bucket of bolts," as his colleague C-3PO calls him. In fact, R2 is an ingenious little droid with useful gadgets and tools that help him to save the day on more than one occasion.

STEP-BY-STEP

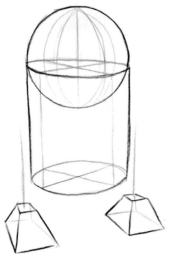

1) R2's body is made up of a cylinder and a sphere. Add pyramids with the tops cut off for his "feet."

2) Add more shapes to give more detail. Erase lines you don't want in your final image.

Radar eye

Holographic projector

3) Add all the little shapes that show off R2's parts, such as his holographic projector, lights, vents, and compartment panels. Don't forget his all-seeing radar eye in the middle of his rotating dome!

EXPERT ADVICE

Unlike humans, droids like R2-D2 don't have limbs and facial features. Look in DK's *Star Wars Visual Dictionary* books to see what all his parts do. The more you know how a droid is built, the easier it will be to draw him!

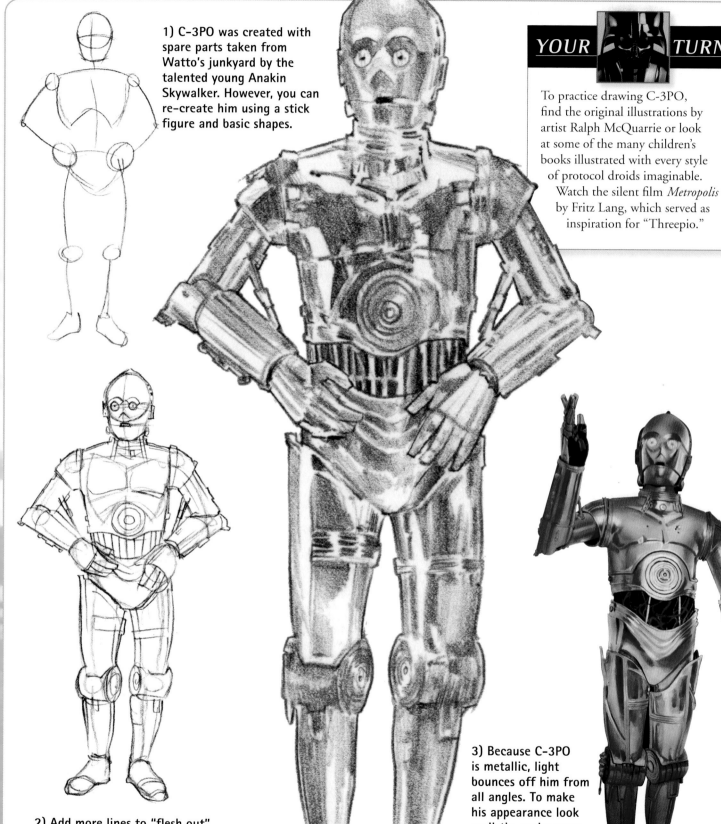

1) C-3PO was created with spare parts taken from Watto's junkyard by the talented young Anakin Skywalker. However, you can re-create him using a stick figure and basic shapes.

YOUR TURN!

To practice drawing C-3PO, find the original illustrations by artist Ralph McQuarrie or look at some of the many children's books illustrated with every style of protocol droids imaginable. Watch the silent film *Metropolis* by Fritz Lang, which served as inspiration for "Threepio."

2) Add more lines to "flesh out" the body and give his joints a robotic appearance. You can add detail to his facial expression.

3) Because C-3PO is metallic, light bounces off him from all angles. To make his appearance look realistic, make areas where reflections would occur lighter.

STEP-BY-STEP

BATTLE DROIDS

"ROGER, ROGER"

These robotic soldiers of the Trade Federation are easily taken down one or two at a time with a mere lightsaber swipe. But when they attack in large numbers, battle droids are an enemy to be reckoned with. The standard B-1 battle droid is tall, lanky, and armed with a blaster. Follow the steps below to build your own droid army.

STEP-BY-STEP

1) Begin sketching a stick figure of the battle droid's body using basic shapes.

2) Add its shin plates and metal body. Modify the blaster and add the backpack.

3) Add more details like the "eye," the backpack's antenna, and shade the blaster.

Clawed hands

Arm extension pistons

High-torque motors

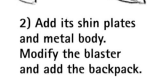

YOUR TURN!

Just like the components in any army, battle droids are specialized for different tasks. By changing the colors and markings on the droids, you can give them different roles. While the infantry battle droid is plain, the pilot droid displays blue markings, and security droids have red markings.

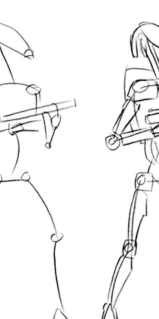

4) Shade and highlight more precise areas of the droid's bone-white metal body to add dimension. Battle droids are designed to look like the skeletons of dead Neimoidians, in order to appear more threatening to the enemy.

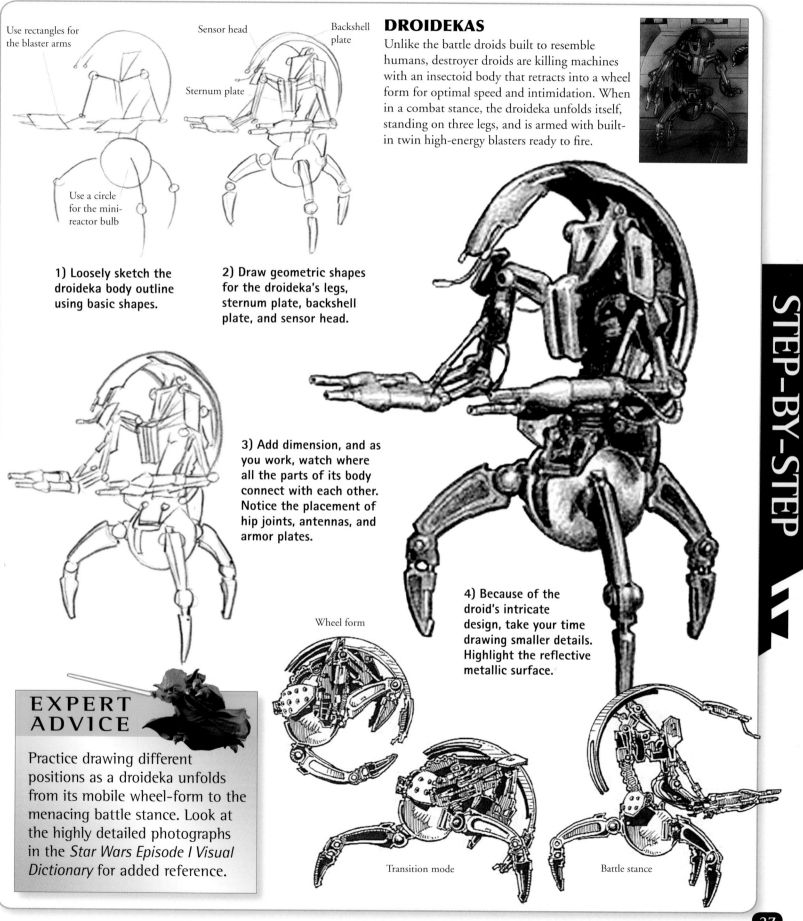

Use rectangles for the blaster arms

Sensor head

Backshell plate

Sternum plate

Use a circle for the mini-reactor bulb

1) Loosely sketch the droideka body outline using basic shapes.

2) Draw geometric shapes for the droideka's legs, sternum plate, backshell plate, and sensor head.

DROIDEKAS

Unlike the battle droids built to resemble humans, destroyer droids are killing machines with an insectoid body that retracts into a wheel form for optimal speed and intimidation. When in a combat stance, the droideka unfolds itself, standing on three legs, and is armed with built-in twin high-energy blasters ready to fire.

3) Add dimension, and as you work, watch where all the parts of its body connect with each other. Notice the placement of hip joints, antennas, and armor plates.

Wheel form

4) Because of the droid's intricate design, take your time drawing smaller details. Highlight the reflective metallic surface.

EXPERT ADVICE

Practice drawing different positions as a droideka unfolds from its mobile wheel-form to the menacing battle stance. Look at the highly detailed photographs in the *Star Wars Episode I Visual Dictionary* for added reference.

Transition mode

Battle stance

STEP-BY-STEP

27

ALIENS

BIZARRE BEINGS

The *Star Wars* galaxy is jam-packed with unusual creatures and fantastical characters. Even though you've been drawing humanoid characters with proportional shapes, now is the time to add height, weight, or in Jabba's case, a lot of belly fat, to give a character its own unique presence.

1) Because Jabba the Hutt is anything but stick-like, loosely sketch his basic shape using circles and curves.

Egg-shaped head

2) Draw a vertical line to keep his facial features symmetrical. Flesh out the rest of his large slug-like body.

Folds of skin cover his neck

Gungans on the Go

Broken into two races, Gungans look either like Jar Jar Binks, from the gangly, orange-skinned Otolla race, or like Boss Nass, from the green-skinned Ankura race. Here we see both travelling in a Naboo jungle.

Mouth takes up half his face

YOUR TURN!

When drawing a character without an obvious skeletal structure, such as Jabba, or oddly proportioned features like the elongated necks of the Kaminoans, visualize the basic shapes of their bodies. Look at real-life animals that may have inspired these alien attributes for more guidance.

Jabba's tail moves like his arms

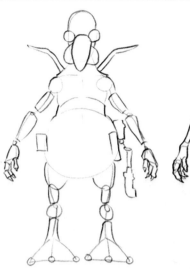

1) Draw the basic shapes of this pudgy Toydarian Watto. Add lines for his hummingbird-like wings.

2) Use a long oval for Watto's flexible nose. Sketch sausage shapes for his arms and legs.

3) Darken lines to emphasize his squinty eyes, three-fingered hands, and webbed feet.

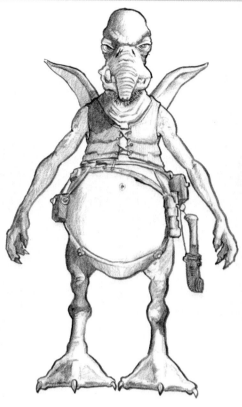

4) Define Watto's facial ridges and snaggle-tooth grimace. Shade his belly to make it appear round.

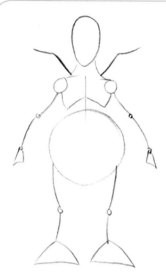

Elderly stance is balanced on a walking stick

Poggle the Lesser is defined by his insectoid body, long facial wattles, and ornate, bejeweled armor and bracelets.

Circles and triangles make up the spidery figure

Acklays scamper quickly on their "fingertips," forming huge, deadly claws.

29

ACTION!

ON THE MOVE

Whether it's a brave Jedi locked in a lightsaber duel with a Sith Lord, or Han Solo running from a crowd of stormtroopers, no *Star Wars* character ever stands still for long. Practice drawing your favorite characters jumping, running, fighting, walking, or even falling. As the action plays out on the page, you'll see the character come to life right before your eyes.

SPLAKOW!

BTEW!

LEAPING LUKE

Watch as Jedi Luke Skywalker springs into action against an unseen enemy. As you draw each stage, pay attention to the placement of his arms and legs.

1) It might appear as though Luke is merely kneeling. However, as the action progresses, it's quite clear that he's getting ready to leap into the air.

2) Luke's clothes shift as he moves, so don't forget to change the folds and wrinkles in his outfit.

ACTION SKETCHBOOK

As you practice drawing various action poses of *Star Wars* characters, experiment with dynamic poses and allow yourself to make some mistakes. That's how you learn! Doodles aren't meant to be masterpieces.

3) Don't get hung up on detail; focus on his actions, not facial expressions.

4) As Luke hits the ground, he is balanced and in control of his movements.

5) With the flow of motion nearing an end, Luke returns to a kneeling position so he is ready to leap into action again.

ACTION DETAILS

TWISTS AND TURNS

Action doesn't begin with the head, arms, or even the legs. In fact, if you start with the limbs and not with the spine, you might get way off track. Always start with the torso and turn it to the side or twist the spine to achieve dynamic poses.

Trunk Rotation

Princess Leia stands defiantly with her torso slightly twisted, revealing a reversed "S" curvature down her spine. Darth Maul, however, exhibits a "C" curve in his central axis as he stands in a defensive pose. While his shoulders align with the curve, Maul's head tilts slightly to the side. His hips remain parallel to the ground, keeping his center of gravity steady.

SPEED LINES

Artists like to use a quick trick to add a sense of immediate movement; they draw simple speed lines behind a character. Here, they are used on a clone trooper as he races by in hot pursuit.

Use an elongated "C" curve to create Lando Calrissian's twisting body.

ASSASSIN STRETCH

Remember that the more unusual the position of your character, the more dynamic the sense of movement will be. As a highly skilled shape-shifting bounty hunter, Zam Wesell uses her entire body to find the right angle on her doomed target.

Horizontal "S" curve

Triangles for feet

Add helmet

Add dimension to Zam's blaster

YOUR TURN!

Try sketching a variety of stick figures using "S" and "C" curves. Decide what kind of movement you'd like the character to do, then add the legs, arm, hands, and feet. The angle of the head also determines the direction the figure is moving.

1) Begin with an elongated horizontal "S" along the axis line. Draw circles and triangles for her head, rear, knees, and the hand gripping the blaster. Triangles represent the other hand and her feet.

2) Add lines to flesh out Zam's muscles as well as the outline of her elastic bodysuit and shin-guard boots.

3) Use the smooth-shading technique to add depth and shadow to the elements of her outfit, which include comlink helmet, wrist-guard gauntlet, blast-energy sink skirt, and shin-guard boots.

STEP-BY-STEP

PERSPECTIVE & BODY PERSPECTIVE

TAKE THE SCENIC ROUTE

To add realism to a scene, you'll need to use the art of perspective. Perspective is the way artists make their drawings look three-dimensional. To learn how to use perspective, first we'll discuss vanishing points and the horizon line.

Horizon

Objects in the distance look smaller than items within your reach. Observe how Han Solo's head is substantially larger than the Tusken Raider's entire body.

Where these guidelines meet is called the vanishing point.

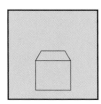

From above, the top of a cube becomes narrower toward the back.

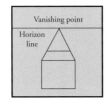

Draw extended lines to see where they would meet on the horizon.

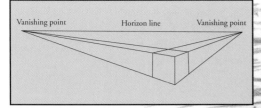

In this example of a two-point perspective, the cube is slightly rotated so we can see three sides. The lines are extended to their "vanishing points," which always sit on the horizon line.

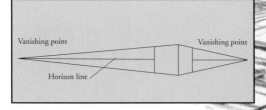

With the top and bottom out of sight, only two sides of the cube extend, but this time the cube sits in the middle of the horizon line.

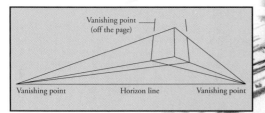

In this example of three-point perspective, the sides of the cube appear to get narrower as they go up. They would eventually meet way up above.

DIFFERENT ANGLES

Once you've mastered the basics of perspective, mix it up by moving around the "camera" angles. After all, when you draw, you're the director. Watching a scene from different angles gives the viewer a more exciting experience than seeing the same action from above.

Shifting the vantage point can add intensity.

Can you find the vanishing point in this one-point perspective of a dramatic duel?

Rotating the view of Darth Maul and Qui-Gon Jinn changes the appearance of their body sizes.

Drawing this scene in three-point perspective adds a feeling of height.

Gaining Perspective

Experiment with different angles to create tension, anticipation, and excitement.

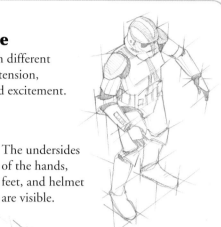

The undersides of the hands, feet, and helmet are visible.

Remember to include details like the top of the helmet from this perspective.

Note the head is smaller than this Jedi's feet.

The opposite is true from this perspective.

FORESHORTENING

GET THE POINT?

As an object is angled toward the viewer it appears shorter than it really is. This is called foreshortening. Point your hand at a mirror. Your arm will actually seem shorter than if you hold it out to the side. Also the pointing hand will look larger than your other hand. Foreshortening is important when creating perspective for any scene.

TUSKEN RAIDER

These sketches of a Tusken Raider in motion best display foreshortening and how it can be used to add drama! See how in the final illustration his left foot seems smaller than the right? His legs aren't different lengths; he's merely standing at an angle to the viewer.

NEED A HAN?

Foreshortening isn't easy, but the more you practice it, the more realistic your illustrations will appear. Visualize your character constructed from basic shapes. Rotate the stick figure in your mind and be observant of his limb placement while he runs, fights, and stands at an angle.

EXPERT ADVICE

When practicing your foreshortening skills, place a wooden artist mannequin or an anatomical model in various action positions to better visualize body shapes in motion.

Notice how the thigh is attached to the rest of his torso

Draw the angle of this leg so it's a bit longer than his back leg

1) Before Han Solo can be a suave blaster-carrying smuggler, he's a stick figure aiming a rectangle!

2) Continue sketching the body, breaking the legs and arms into cylinders connected by spherical joints.

Notice how Han's blaster appears to be leaping off the page

Observe the difference between Jedi Aayla Secura's back leg and arm compared to the ones featured in front of the sketch.

3) Once the foreshortened form is finalized, add clothes. Be aware of the light source when adding his shadow to the background.

STEP-BY-STEP

ANAKIN

Born into slavery, trained as a Jedi, and later transformed into a Sith Lord, Anakin Skywalker is familiar with both sides of the Force. Possessing more midi-chlorians than even Jedi Master Yoda, Anakin has remarkable powers. However, he is a character in emotional turmoil. His conflicting loyalties to the Jedi, Padmé, Obi-Wan Kenobi, and Chancellor Palpatine are written all over his angst-ridden face.

LEAVING HOME

Winning his freedom in a Podrace opened doors for the young Skywalker. However, his complete devotion to his mother Shmi makes his decision to leave very difficult (see above). Training at the Jedi Temple means he must abandon his mother. When she is killed by Tusken Raiders, Anakin proves that he is capable of ruthless violence when he exacts his revenge.

CHARACTER HISTORY

Anakin and his mother Shmi lived as slaves, owned by the Toydarian junk dealer Watto on Tatooine. During his time in the shop, Anakin learned to fix anything mechanical and built his own protocol droid—C-3PO. Though young Anakin's mechanical and racing skills were more than impressive, his grasp of the Force led Jedi Master Qui-Gon Jinn to believe he was the Chosen One of the prophecy. Training under Jedi Master Obi-Wan Kenobi, Anakin learned to hone his Jedi skills but never quite mastered how to keep his emotions in check. Chancellor Palpatine saw this character flaw as a way to later manipulate the impetuous Jedi in his devious plan to rule the galaxy. With fear and suspicion ruling Anakin's thoughts, he eventually turned on his Jedi brethren including Obi-Wan, sacrificing his human side to become Darth Vader.

"LIKE A JEDI HE IS ALWAYS WILLING TO PUT HIMSELF AT RISK TO HELP OTHERS"

EXPERT ADVICE

Anakin may wear his heart on his sleeve, but more than one emotion hides behind those piercing eyes. When drawing Anakin, decide first if you want to portray him as loving, suspicious, concerned, joyous, or angry. Always keep in mind *why* he is feeling that way. Show the emotion in his face (see page 47) but also use different cues in his body language such as his stance and head tilt.

This loose sketch of Anakin Skywalker uses circles for muscle joints and his skull, and rectangles for muscles and basic body shapes. The spine uses a subtle "S" curve to twist the torso. Use your foreshortening skills to achieve the correct body proportions. Make sure you get this right before fleshing out the figure.

This loose sketch of Anakin Skywalker uses circles for muscle joints and his skull, and rectangles for muscles and basic body shapes. The spine uses a subtle "S" curve to twist the torso. Use your foreshortening skills to achieve the correct body proportions. Make sure you get this right before fleshing out the figure.

FINAL PENCIL DRAWING

After defining the muscle tone, dress him! Fit Anakin in his usual Jedi Knight garb, complete with a dark tunic, pants, belt, and boots. Add highlights to Anakin's shaggy hair so it doesn't appear flat.

Place a shadow on the left side of Anakin's face for dramatic effect.

Draw lines throughout the clothing for realistic wrinkles.

SPEED PODRACER

Anakin's super-fast reflexes powered by Force-intuition make him a masterful Podracer, as he often sees events before they occur. His racing talents lead him to drive on behalf of visiting Jedi Master Qui-Gon Jinn and Anakin's future wife, Padmé Amidala. His piloting skills make him a hero during the Clone Wars, especially when he successfully rescues Chancellor Palpatine. Practice drawing Anakin in different vehicles, testing his piloting skills to the max.

DUEL PERSONALITY

Wielding his lightsaber against such opponents as the droid army, Count Dooku, and ultimately his own mentor, Obi-Wan, Anakin's skills with a lightsaber earn him a reputation as a talented warrior. Originally fighting on the side of justice, Anakin fights bravely against the Republic's enemies, but later, at the insistence of Palpatine, he mercilessly strikes down a defenseless Count Dooku. However, his duels are not without risk. Anakin's hand is severed during an earlier fight with Count Dooku, and his remaining limbs are lost in the bloody Mustafar duel against Obi-Wan.

FORBIDDEN LOVE

As a young boy, Anakin harbored an innocent crush on Padmé Amidala. Anakin crosses her path again when he is assigned to protect the beautiful Senator from assassination attempts. Their mutual affection grows and as Jedi are not permitted to marry, the two eventually wed in secret, as shown in the illustration above. Although initially happy, nightmares of his beloved dying during childbirth continually torment Anakin. These prophetic visions drive him to seek power from the dark side. Try to capture Anakin's devotion to Padmé when drawing them together.

FINAL INK DRAWING

Heavily ink Anakin's dark wardrobe and add parallel lines to his pants and undergarments for contrast. Utilize white space to indicate reflections of the light source. Use the stippling technique (drawing multiple dots) around the lightsaber blade so that it appears to sizzle!

Remember finer details like the glove on Anakin's mechanical hand.

Use thin ink lines to lightly shade his robes.

CLONE WARS

For the most dynamic setting, place one character in hot pursuit of another, or place them head-to-head in the throes of battle. This Manga comic-style illustration uses heavily inked outlines and bold colors to give a more animated feeling to the fight scene.

THE HEAD

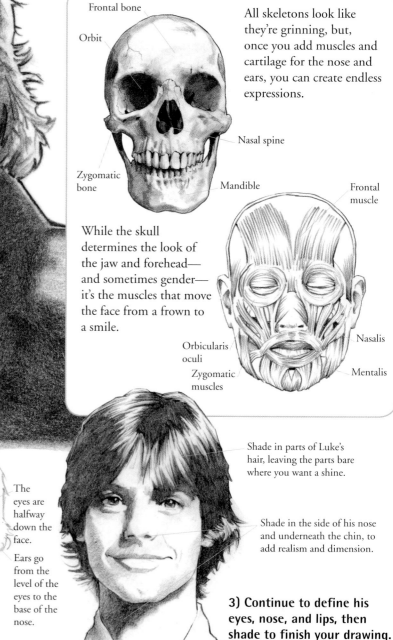

ABOUT FACE!

The emotion and true nature of a character comes from his or her face. Follow these basic steps to best convey how your character feels. Pay close attention to all aspects of the face from the furrowed brow to laughter lines around the eyes.

Frontal bone

Orbit

All skeletons look like they're grinning, but, once you add muscles and cartilage for the nose and ears, you can create endless expressions.

Nasal spine

Zygomatic bone

Mandible

Frontal muscle

While the skull determines the look of the jaw and forehead— and sometimes gender— it's the muscles that move the face from a frown to a smile.

Orbicularis oculi

Zygomatic muscles

Nasalis

Mentalis

How can we tell if Luke Skywalker feels a disturbance in the Force, if we don't see concern expressed on his face?

The base of the nose is halfway between the eyes and the chin.

The eyes are halfway down the face.

Ears go from the level of the eyes to the base of the nose.

Shade in parts of Luke's hair, leaving the parts bare where you want a shine.

Shade in the side of his nose and underneath the chin, to add realism and dimension.

1) Sketch a loose oval for the skull and strong lines toward the bottom for the jaw. Draw guidelines to place facial features.

2) Start to lightly sketch in Luke's eyes, nose, and mouth where you placed your horizontal guidelines.

3) Continue to define his eyes, nose, and lips, then shade to finish your drawing.

NON-HUMAN HEADS

Not all heads are built alike. And in a galaxy far, far away, you can bet there will be more than one memorable mug. Some aliens, such as the Bith, have smooth foreheads that never seem to end, while other aliens, like the Mon Calamari Admiral Ackbar, have eyes on the far sides of their skulls.

1) Use basic shapes to sketch the rough outline of this unusual head. Note that the facial features are all in the center of the head.

Shade the face to show the mottled skin patterns.

2) By adding wrinkles to the skin and the finer facial details, including the protruding eyes, the Mon Calamari's profile comes to life.

3) Most Mon Calamari have salmon-colored skin, although some have blue and silver skin. Keep this in mind as you shade.

Gills mean Mon Calmaris can stay underwater for long periods of time.

YOUR TURN!

When drawing a lobster-like domed head of the Mon Calamari or the slender ridged face of an Utapaun, take special care to accent the differences in each species you draw. In these pictures, for example, notice the placement of the razor-sharp teeth of Tion Medon.

As you draw the intimidating character Tion Medon, make note of his gaunt, pale face and sunken black eyes. Even his lack of expression speaks volumes.

The vertical folds in Tion's regal collar echo his distinct facial lines.

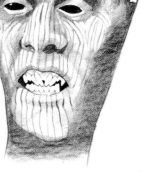

MALE HEAD

TAKE IT AT FACE VALUE

He may be called a scruffy looking nerf herder, but here Han Solo looks more like a handsome swashbuckler. Now that you understand the basics of drawing a head, it's time to learn the finer details of drawing a classic male face complete with chiselled jaw line, strong nose, and prominent chin.

Male Details

Typically a male character has bushy eyebrows, big facial features, and a full bottom lip. And unlike female characters, male eyelashes are shorter.

Eyes

Draw a basic circle for the eyeball with a smaller circle inside that for the pupil. Add an oval around the pupil to form the eyelid. Add short eyelashes to finish.

Front Male Head

To keep Han's face in proportion, draw a grid—which is a more elaborate extension of the horizontal and vertical guidelines—to help you decide where to put the eyes, nose, ears, mouth, and chin.

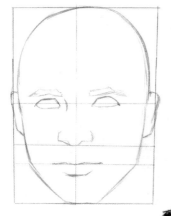

1) After sketching the oval shape for the face, lightly draw a rectangular shape as an outline. Draw a vertical line through the middle. Draw three horizontal lines to represent the eyes, nose, and mouth. The eyes should be halfway down the oval.

2) As you refine every aspect of Han's face, make sure that features on both sides of the vertical line are balanced.

Nose

Sketch a thin, long rectangle for the base of the nose with triangles below for a three-dimensional effect. As you smooth the lines, the nostrils will become more apparent.

Mouth

Continue using basic shapes, such as long, horizontal rectangles with triangular edges, to form the mouth. Use crosshatching to soften the lines and make the lips more lifelike.

STEP-BY-STEP

FACIAL EXPRESSIONS

Whether Han Solo is outrunning the Empire in the *Millennium Falcon* or telling someone to silence C-3PO, you can rest assured he doesn't have a poker face. As you draw Han, or any other character bursting with emotion, observe how his eyes squint when he's confident or how wrinkles develop in the forehead when he's afraid.

DETERMINED

FEARFUL

CONFIDENT

Profile Male Head

Just as before, use a grid to help keep the eyes, nose, mouth, and chin in proper perspective. Because this is a profile portrait, don't neglect sometimes forgotten elements like the ears.

Male Details

As you sketch, notice the strong jaw-line, as well as a more prominent chin on the male, and, if he's too busy to shave, stubble. Keep in mind this applies to humanoid characters. Female Ewoks and Wookiees tend to be just as furry as the males!

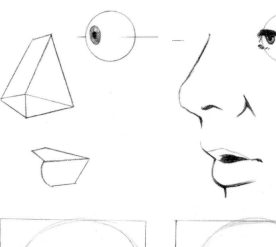

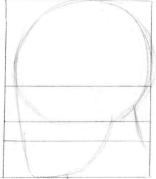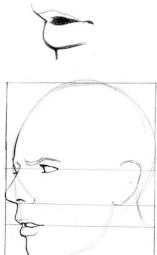

STEP-BY-STEP

1) Lightly sketch the head using basic shapes. The nose and ears should be on the same guideline.

2) Begin adding facial features. Because he is drawn at an angle, you won't see them in their entirety.

3) In the final step, shade the eyes, nose, hair, mouth, jaw, chin and cheekbone for more depth, and add dimension and style to his hair. Don't forget his shirt collar and jacket!

FEMALE HEAD

A THING OF BEAUTY

Even though the female face has properties similar to those of a male, the features should be softer and more feminine. Many female characters, especially Padmé Amidala, have hair that can be styled numerous ways, which in turn adds more interest to their overall look.

Female Details

Typically a woman has shaped eyebrows, long eyelashes, a small nose and ears, and full lips. The cheekbones may also be more pronounced than a man's.

Eyes

Draw a basic circle for the eyeball with a smaller circle inside for the pupil. Add an oval for the eyelid. Lightly sketch curvy eyelashes on the upper and lower lids.

Front Female Head

Use a grid to keep Padmé's face in proportion. The horizontal and vertical guidelines show exactly where to place the character's eyes, nose, ears, mouth, and chin.

1) Sketch an oval shape for a face, and lightly draw a triangle for the chin. Draw a vertical line through the rectangle to keep the eyes symmetrical. Draw three horizontal lines for the eyebrows, eyes, nose, and mouth.

2) As you add more delicate features to Padmé's face, be careful not to overdo it. Her shapely eyebrows only arch slightly over her eyes, and her lips are full but not too heavily shaded. As you draw in her eyelashes, don't add too many! She should look naturally beautiful.

Nose

Sketch a thin, shorter rectangle for the base of the nose with more angular triangles for the bottom. The ideal nose for Padmé is thin and narrow. But be aware that each nose is different.

Mouth

Use the same basic shapes of long rectangles with triangular edges to form the mouth. Make them a bit taller than male lips and shade them so that they are fuller and softer looking.

FACIAL EXPRESSIONS

Whether Padmé is arguing on behalf of her home world Naboo in the Senate or confessing her love to Anakin Skywalker, she never keeps the same expression for long. As you draw Padmé, notice how her mouth is slightly parted when she's surprised and at a loss for words, or how her otherwise calm brows are distinctly angled when she's outraged.

SURPRISED

SADNESS

ANGER

Profile Female Head

Use this grid to help keep Padmé's eyes, nose, mouth, and chin in the right place. As it is a profile portrait, you won't see her entire face.

Female Details

As you sketch, notice the softer jaw line, as well as a smaller chin than the male's. Her ears will be smaller, too.

STEP-BY-STEP

1) Start with basic shapes to sketch Padmé's profile. Horizontal lines show where her facial features will go.

2) Add a dainty nose, a full-lipped mouth, large eyes, groomed brows, and small ears. Align the nose and ear.

3) In the final step, keep her complexion smooth and even as you shade. Add shine to her perfectly coiffed hairstyle. Make the eyelashes lush and add slightly dark shading to the upper lip to add depth.

HANDS

HIGH FIVE

Just as the face expresses a wide array of emotions, hand gestures can also drive a point home. Hands can be one of the most difficult parts of the body to draw, so study sketches by art masters such as Leonardo da Vinci.

Having mastered the art of using Sith lightning, Count Dooku's hands are formidable weapons. In this picture his hands are the main focus point.

HAND STRUCTURE

Not all *Star Wars* hands are as Force-sensitive as Count Dooku's, but most have four fingers, an opposable thumb, and a palm. While a female's hand is slender with shapely fingernails, a male's hand is larger with protruding knuckles and bigger fingers. Examine illustrations of skeletons to understand bone structure better.

Female hand

Male hand

Metacarpal bones

Hamate

Carpal bones

Scaphoid

Ulna

Radius

HANDS UP!

When drawing a hand, use the basic shapes of squares, rectangles, and cylinders.

The top of the thumb lines up with the base of the fingers.

1) Draw a rough square for the palm of the hand. A vertical line indicates the wrist.

2) Draw light vertical lines above the square to represent the positions of the fingers and thumb.

3) Flesh out the hand. Make the fingers from cylinders and use circles for the parts of the palm.

4) Shade the skin. Add wrinkles where the fingers and wrist bend, and lines on the palm.

GRIP

Depending on what the hand is holding, its shape can vary. A hand holding a thermal detonator is quite different from a hand grasping a lightsaber. Some hands don't even have muscle and skin, such as Anakin's robotic one.

ALIEN LIMBS

While Luke, Han, and other humanoid characters have the usual limbs, hands, and feet, others in the *Star Wars* galaxy exhibit rather exotic, and sometimes advantageous, appendages. Have fun drawing different physical attributes in alien species and characters, whether it's the suction-cupped fingertips of the Rodian Greedo or the intimidating lethorns of Chagrian Mas Amedda.

YOUR TURN!

Be brave! Dive right in and draw characters with the most ambitious appendages such as the multi-armed General Grievous or the long limbs and fingers of the Troiken podracer, Gasgano. Look at books and comics for reference images or use action figures as highly-detailed artist models.

Add shading to create bumps in the skull.

Make his fingernails sharp and pointy!

Let his lekku (head tail) drape across his shoulders.

TWI'LEKS

The most distinctive feature of Twi'leks is a pair of long, shapely tentacles that grow from the base of the skull and wrap around the shoulders. The lekku of Twi'leks, like those of Jedi Knight Aayla Secura, move gracefully.

Claws are rarely bared unless in battle.

YODA'S HANDS

Grasping either his ever-present gimer stick or a green-bladed lightsaber, Yoda's expressive hands are hard not to notice. His highly tuned powers can defeat nearly any opponent instantly.

Hand gestures help Yoda concentrate while using the Force.

GEONOSIAN

The insect-like Geonosian soldier drone not only has an elongated face and flexible multi-jointed limbs, they also have outer and inner wings reminiscent of a large dragonfly's. This drone grasps his sonic blaster with two fingers and a thumb.

Loosely sketch the long wings on your Geonosian stick figure. Also draw his powerful, pronged footclaws.

Fine lines add depth and texture

SARLACC

Start with a series of overlapping circles and then fill in the smaller details of the tentacles and sharp rows of teeth.

EXPERT ADVICE

As you practice drawing alien limbs, visualize their purpose. Do they help the character eat, walk, or fight? The more you know about a character's anatomy, the easier it will be to draw him or her in action.

CLOTHING & ARMOR

READY-TO-WEAR

After drawing bodies for your characters, you get to dress them! The style of clothing and color choice can reveal a great deal about their profession and personality. After all, what's Darth Vader without his signature black cape or a stormtrooper without his white armor?

FORCE FASHIONS

When a character moves, so does his clothing. As you draw Obi-Wan Kenobi's tunic or Mace Windu's floor-length robe, take special care to shade darker lines for folds in the fabric. Creases often form at stress points in the fabric like where the arms bend.

A lot of *Star Wars'* characters, such as this Red Guard, wear long draping material.

EXPERT ADVICE

Clothes reflect and absorb light depending on the fabric. Velvet and silk react differently to light than leather and wool. As you shade and highlight wrinkles in the fabric consider the costume's materials.

REGAL RUNWAY

Padmé Amidala is never one to dress down. Each costume she wears reveals part of her personality. One dress mirrors her flirtatious mood while another demure gown matches her serious mood. The traditional throne-room gown shows her commitment to her role as Queen of Naboo.

ARMED & STYLISH

The stark sleekness of this white armor conveys the cold and unfeeling characteristics of a stormtrooper. Made of plastoid composite, the armor should be drawn in sections as opposed to one single piece.

Sketch this stormtrooper starting with a stick figure and basic cylindrical shapes. Shade the black fabric of the body glove worn underneath the armor.

STEP-BY-STEP

DARTH VADER

As the infamous Dark Lord of the Sith, Darth Vader can simply breathe and it will send chills down the spines of both his troops and his enemies. His ability to crush his victims with his mind means that Darth Vader is one of the most feared agents of the Empire. His Force powers and his allegiance to the Emperor make him a legendary villain and the ultimate foe to the Rebel Alliance.

MAN OF MYSTERY

Although we know that Darth Vader is a cyborg created from the wounded body of Anakin Skywalker, the inhuman black mask, thick black armor, and draping cape give him a brand new identity. As a ruthless enforcer of Emperor Palpatine's rule across the galaxy, Darth Vader relies upon his terrifying visage and reputation to invoke fear and respect. No part of his body is left uncovered by the expanse of black clothing and armor. His monumental figure towers over almost everyone he encounters. His new lightsaber has a crimson blade, which is powered by a synthetic crystal, supplied by Darth Sidious.

CHARACTER HISTORY

Seduced by the dark side of the Force, Jedi Knight Anakin Skywalker sacrifices his identity and is renamed Darth Vader by Emperor Palpatine, aka Darth Sidious. Under the Emperor's orders, he helps to eliminate all the Jedi inside their temple, including the inexperienced younglings. In a heated argument, he Force-chokes his beloved wife Padmé—which leads to her death. A lightsaber duel against his mentor Obi-Wan Kenobi results in the loss of his limbs—as well as severe body damage from lava burns—forcing him to live the rest of his life as a cyborg. Years later, Darth Vader would not only duel one last time against Ben Kenobi, but also against his own son, Luke Skywalker.

EXPERT ADVICE

As you practice drawing Darth Vader, pay close attention to all facets of his appearance. Notice the folds and texture of his cape and clothing. Shade his helmet to showcase its reflective qualities. Practice drawing him in dynamic action-poses and use his body language to convey emotion, since his face is hidden beneath the ominous black mask.

ROUGH PENCIL DRAWING

Before starting, think of how Darth Vader's stance will help express the mood of the piece. Give him a threatening pose as he stretches out his hand. As usual, start with basic shapes like circles, squares, rectangles, and triangles.

Before starting, think of how Darth Vader's stance will help express the mood of the piece. Give him a threatening pose as he stretches out his hand. As usual, start with basic shapes like circles, squares, rectangles, and triangles.

FINAL PENCIL DRAWING

Further define Darth Vader's helmet, armor, clothing, and lightsaber hilt. Because he's dressed all in black, proper shading is crucial. Determine the direction of the light source reflecting off his helmet, then use shading techniques to indicate where the illustration should be heavily inked.

"X" marks the areas where you need heavy shading.

Leave blank the areas where reflections will occur.

DETAILS

MAN VS. MACHINE

Due to the massive injuries he sustained on Mustafar, Darth Vader depends on mechanical limbs to move and a cybernetic life support system to breathe. He wears a helmet and protective armor at all times (except when he is in his healing chamber). Appearing more like a robot than a man, he strikes fear into the hearts of Rebel enemies as well as his own troops. Having little or no sympathy for others, his reputation is that of a cruel, unfeeling cyborg. With the remainder of his body maimed and scarred—including a broken heart—Darth Vader's humanity is almost non-existent. It is only when Luke Skywalker removes the helmet of the dying Darth Vader that we glimpse the man he once was.

TECHNICAL WIZARD

The young Anakin Skywalker created and restored the verbose protocol droid C-3PO from scrap metal to help his mother Shmi with her work on Tatooine. The complaint-prone droid watched Anakin mourn the loss of his mother, fall in love with Padmé, and succumb to the power of the dark side. Unfortunately, any evidence of C-3PO's parentage would be lost thanks a memory wipe ordered by Bail Organa shortly after the birth of Luke and Leia. Vader, however, recognizes his old creation in this comic-book scene from *The Empire Strikes Back*.

LEGENDARY WARRIOR

When Darth Vader ignites his red lightsaber, the duel ahead is anything but dull. His ability to Force-choke anyone who dares question his authority with a mere flick of the wrist has made him notorious. Though feared throughout the galaxy, his tactical insights and his desire to be present on the frontlines earn him the undying loyalty of his troops who follow him into battle. His legendary and unmatched piloting skills have garnered respect throughout the Imperial forces and inspired terror in the Empire's foes.

PARTICULARLY--

FINAL INK DRAWING

He's not called the Dark Lord of the Sith for nothing! Heavily ink your portrait of Darth Vader, not only to show off his dark clothing and armor but also his dark demeanor. Let the white space represent reflections and show his ignited lightsaber.

Give the lightsaber a thin ink outline to indicate the blade.

These dark shadows give the character depth.

WEAPONS

LIGHTSABERS

While these elegant weapons are as unique as their Jedi and Sith makers, all lightsabers have a basic structure of a polished metallic hilt (handle), an "on" button, and extra control buttons. When activated, the lightsaber has a powerful beam of energy (around a meter long), which can cut through almost anything.

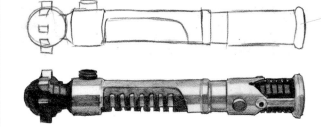

Obi-Wan's first lightsaber is a simple cylinder with a sphere on the end.

Darth Maul's lightsaber is double bladed.

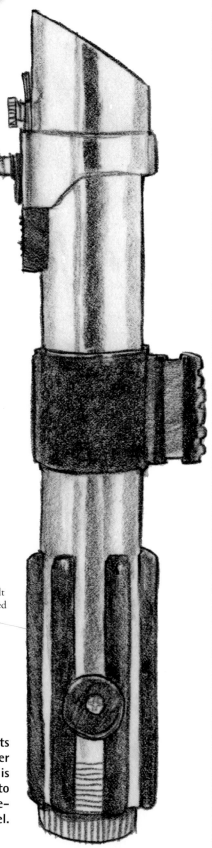

Count Dooku's lightsaber has a curved hilt.

1) Draw a cylinder with a slanting top edge. Use rectangles, squares, and circles to complete the basic shape.

2) Add dimension to the hilt, then detail to the control buttons, and darken the lines you want to keep.

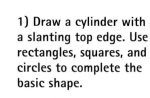

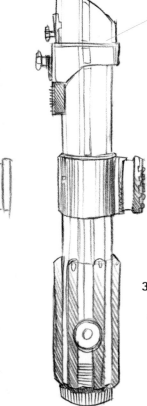

Slanting top edge.

Simple hilt with ridged handle.

ANAKIN'S LIGHTSABER

Anakin Skywalker's lightsaber is less about decoration and more about effectiveness. This makes it easier to sketch the hilt using basic shapes like circles, rectangles, and squares.

3) Shade the parts of the lightsaber where the light is not reflected, to give it a three-dimensional feel.

Notice the basic shapes that create the slender medium-range barrel and sleek grip of Queen Amidala's royal pistol (right). In contrast to Amidala's demur weapon is the multi-functional Security S-5 blaster used by the Naboo Royal Palace Guard (below). Stacked cylinders and rectangles make up the basic shapes of this weapon.

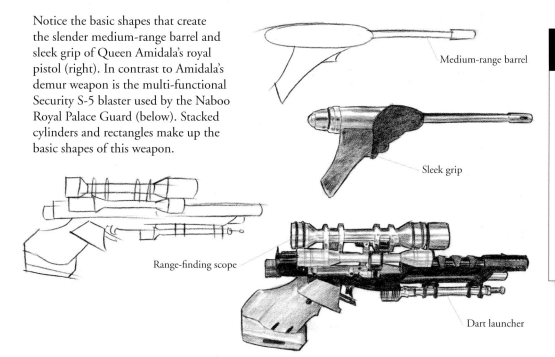

Medium-range barrel

Sleek grip

Range-finding scope

Dart launcher

YOUR TURN!

When Han Solo says to Luke, "Hokey religions and ancient weapons are no match for a good blaster at your side, kid," he had a point. Try drawing characters holding onto various blasters. How does a stormtrooper hold his blaster differently from Queen Amidala? Experiment by sketching characters with weapons that they don't normally use.

STORMTROOPER BLASTER

The Imperial forces may be lousy shots but at least their blasters are impressive. The E-11 BlastTech standard Imperial sidearm is a stormtrooper's most reliable weapon.

1) Roughly sketch the rectangles and squares that make up the basic shape of the stormtrooper blaster. Add the grip and trigger.

Folding three-position stock

2) Darken lines to define smaller features on the blaster, such as the folding three-position stock, the power cell, and the accessory mounting rail.

3) Finally shade the entire weapon using varying levels of shadow and light to reveal the shine from the metal. Transform the shapes into more realistic blaster components.

STEP-BY-STEP

VEHICLES

REV YOUR ENGINES

The vehicles in *Star Wars* are often completely different from anything you would find in everyday life. By following the rules of perspective and shading, however, you can recreate these amazing craft. Use your imagination to invent some weird and wonderful vehicles of your own!

The control pod is much smaller than the engines that power the Podracer.

Split-X radiators make Sebulba's Podracer easy to spot from a distance.

Ben Quadinaros's Podracer has four engines.

At the Boonta Eve Classic on Tatooine every Podracer is as unique as its pilot. The typical Podracer construction, though, is a small cockpit with large and multiple engines—these machines are built for speed!

ANAKIN'S PODRACER

Cylinders and spheres make up young Anakin Skywalker's Podracer. Be sure to get the perspective right before you start filling in the detail.

Use simple cylinders for the engines.

Air scoops

1) Loosely sketch the basic shapes of the Radon Ulzer engines, the control cables, and control pod on Anakin's Podracer.

2) Add triangles for fenders on the control pod, and rectangles on the engines for the air scoops.

3) Add the final details to the cables, engines, and also the blazing effects when the craft is in motion.

AT-ST

The All Terrain Scout Transport (AT-ST)—often referred to as the Scout Walker or Chicken Walker!—is faster and more easily maneuverable than its larger cousin the AT-AT.

Gyro System

Add the command viewport here.

3) Finalize the illustration by adding the rest of the details, and then shade to add dimension.

Twin blaster cannons

Darker shading on the inside of the leg gives the AT-ST depth.

1) Draw a large cube-like shape for the command cabin, a rectangle for the Gyro System, and more rectangles for its legs.

2) Add the twin blaster cannons, knee and ankle joints, shield, and fence-cutting blade at the footpads.

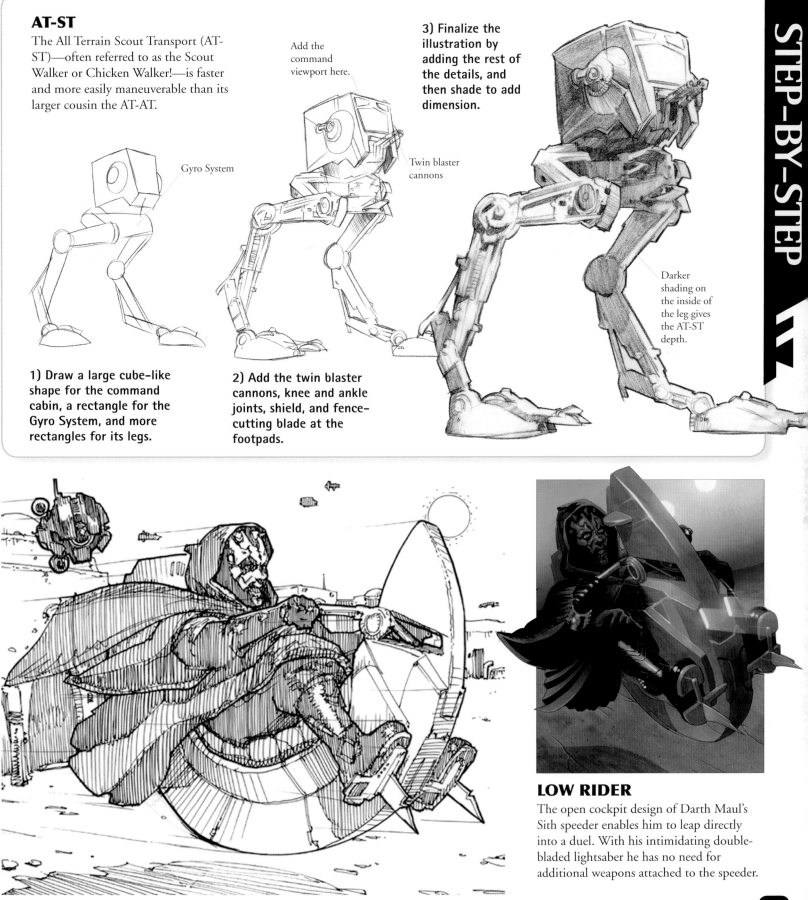

LOW RIDER

The open cockpit design of Darth Maul's Sith speeder enables him to leap directly into a duel. With his intimidating double-bladed lightsaber he has no need for additional weapons attached to the speeder.

STARSHIPS

FLYING THE UNFRIENDLY SKIES

The starships that appear in the *Star Wars* saga have become as recognizable as Darth Vader, Yoda, and Obi-Wan Kenobi. Whether it's the unusual hexagonal shape of a TIE fighter or the symmetry of a T-65 X-wing, every *Star Wars* spacecraft has its own unique design and identity.

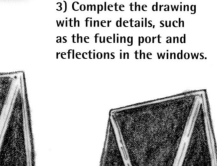

3) Complete the drawing with finer details, such as the fueling port and reflections in the windows.

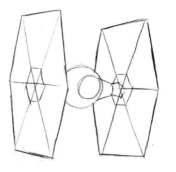

Heavily shade the solar array panels.

1) Sketch the wide panels of the solar array wings, as well as the olive-shaped cockpit.

2) Add the solar array support-frames and the cockpit windows to give the image more depth.

X-Wing Marks the Spot

To fight off Imperial fighters, Rebel pilots fly the T-65 X-wing, complete with long-range laser cannons, proton torpedoes, defensive shields, hyperdrive, and an astromech droid for in-flight repairs.

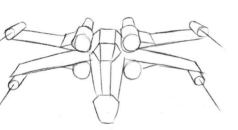

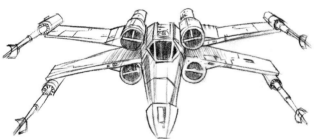

1) Using rectangle, triangle, and circle shapes, lightly sketch the outline of the ship. Keep both sides symmetrical.

2) Continue to add more detail and dimension to the drawing. Use elongated cylinders for the laser cannons.

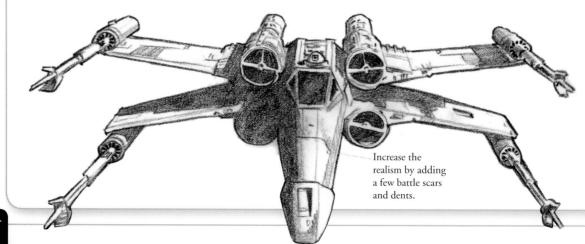

Increase the realism by adding a few battle scars and dents.

3) Begin shading the wings and darken the cockpit area. Don't forget to add an astromech droid co-pilot, such as R2-D2.

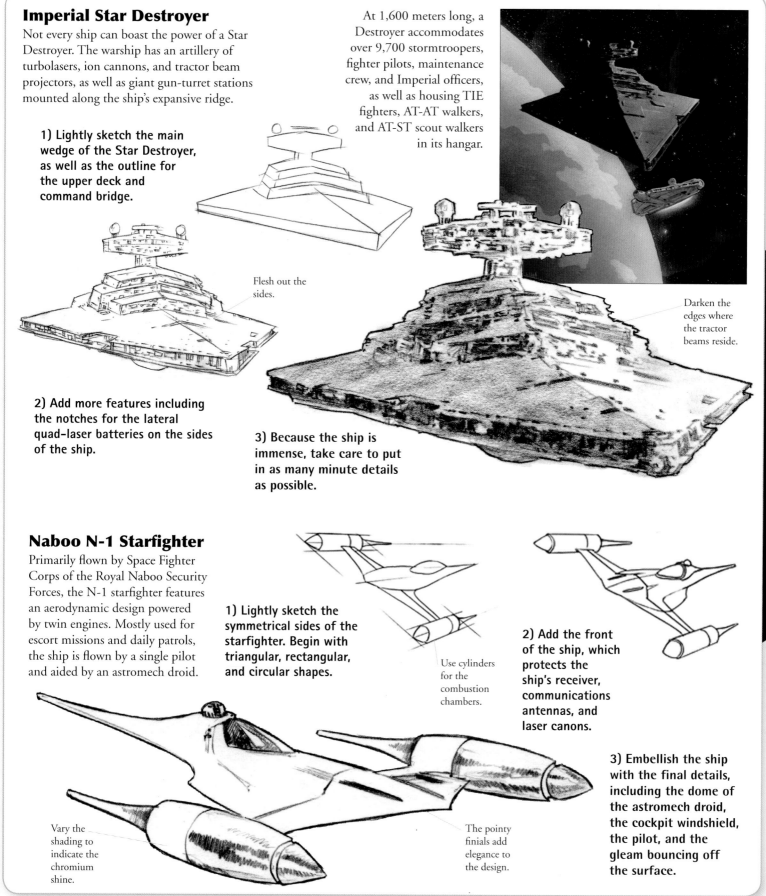

Imperial Star Destroyer

Not every ship can boast the power of a Star Destroyer. The warship has an artillery of turbolasers, ion cannons, and tractor beam projectors, as well as giant gun-turret stations mounted along the ship's expansive ridge.

At 1,600 meters long, a Destroyer accommodates over 9,700 stormtroopers, fighter pilots, maintenance crew, and Imperial officers, as well as housing TIE fighters, AT-AT walkers, and AT-ST scout walkers in its hangar.

1) Lightly sketch the main wedge of the Star Destroyer, as well as the outline for the upper deck and command bridge.

Flesh out the sides.

Darken the edges where the tractor beams reside.

2) Add more features including the notches for the lateral quad-laser batteries on the sides of the ship.

3) Because the ship is immense, take care to put in as many minute details as possible.

Naboo N-1 Starfighter

Primarily flown by Space Fighter Corps of the Royal Naboo Security Forces, the N-1 starfighter features an aerodynamic design powered by twin engines. Mostly used for escort missions and daily patrols, the ship is flown by a single pilot and aided by an astromech droid.

1) Lightly sketch the symmetrical sides of the starfighter. Begin with triangular, rectangular, and circular shapes.

Use cylinders for the combustion chambers.

2) Add the front of the ship, which protects the ship's receiver, communications antennas, and laser canons.

3) Embellish the ship with the final details, including the dome of the astromech droid, the cockpit windshield, the pilot, and the gleam bouncing off the surface.

Vary the shading to indicate the chromium shine.

The pointy finials add elegance to the design.

STEP-BY-STEP

STAR BATTLES

No *Star Wars* film is complete without an exciting aerial battle featuring enormous warships and super-fast starfighters. You can focus on one ship as the prominent element of a panel (see inset) or create a full page packed with a multitude of ships seen at various distances.

MILLENNIUM FALCON

As the fastest "hunk of junk" in the galaxy, the *Millennium Falcon* has served well pilot Han Solo and his Wookiee first mate, Chewbacca, on many adventures. The Falcon's detailed appearance requires patience to draw correctly. But once you have sketched the basic shape, you can build up your *Falcon* step by step to capture all the various features on the ship's surface.

EXPERT ADVICE

Drawing the ship may seem daunting, but the *Falcon* is easy to draw if you look at it piece by piece. The main hull has a saucer shape with elongated rectangles. Positioned on the ship's side is a short cylindrical cockpit. The windows are a series of squares and rectangles, while circles serve as vents and the radar.

MEET THE PILOT

After winning the *Falcon* in an exciting sabacc game against gambler Lando Calrissian, Han Solo used the modified ship to smuggle spices for the dangerous gangster Jabba the Hutt. The *Falcon* was later hired by Ben Kenobi and Luke Skywalker in order to rescue Princess Leia. While the ship seems to be in constant repair, Solo never doubts her worth.

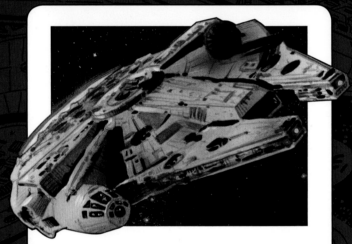

CATCH ME IF YOU CAN

The *Millennium Falcon* is specially modified with military-class quad laser turrets, an antipersonnel repeating laser, concussion missile launchers, and numerous scanner-proof hidden compartments. All these additions are tricky to re-create so try studying the films, books, comics, and cartoons so you can get all these details right. Remember that you can break everything down into basic shapes at first, then add shading and detail once you are happy with the perspective.

VEHICLE HISTORY

Under Lando's ownership, the Corellian Engineering Corporation YT-1300 stock light freighter began its long line of modifications and shield upgrades. It also earned a rather large tear near its entry ramp, thanks to an aggressive Renatasian Confederation starfighter. Later Solo added "borrowed" weaponry and powerful sensor jammers to protect the *Falcon* during combat. As the ship that made the Kessel run in less than 12 parsecs, the *Falcon* has an impressive speed and defense capabilities. When you are drawing the ship in combat, remember that—thanks to all these modifications—the *Falcon* always seems to get away, whether it's down to the unreliable hyperdrive or Han Solo's piloting skills.

The design for the *Millennium Falcon* is based on a hamburger! As you sketch the shape of the craft, notice the flat round shape of the main body, the pincer-shaped front, and the outrigger cockpit that looks suspiciously like an olive!

The design for the Millennium Falcon is based on a hamburger! As you sketch the shape of the craft, notice the flat round shape of the main body, the pincer-shaped front, and the outrigger cockpit that looks suspiciously like an olive!

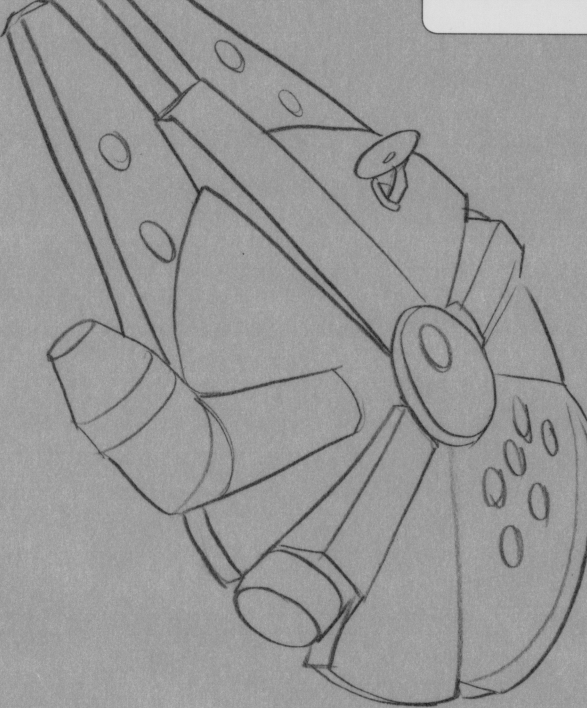

FINAL PENCIL DRAWING

It's time to add the details that make the *Falcon* more than a "big bucket of bolts." To help you draw the ship as accurately as possible—including the gun turret, the wide stabilizer fin, and the shield generators—refer to DK's *Star Wars Incredible Cross-Sections* book.

Drawing with a harder lead pencil will help prevent smudges on the drawing.

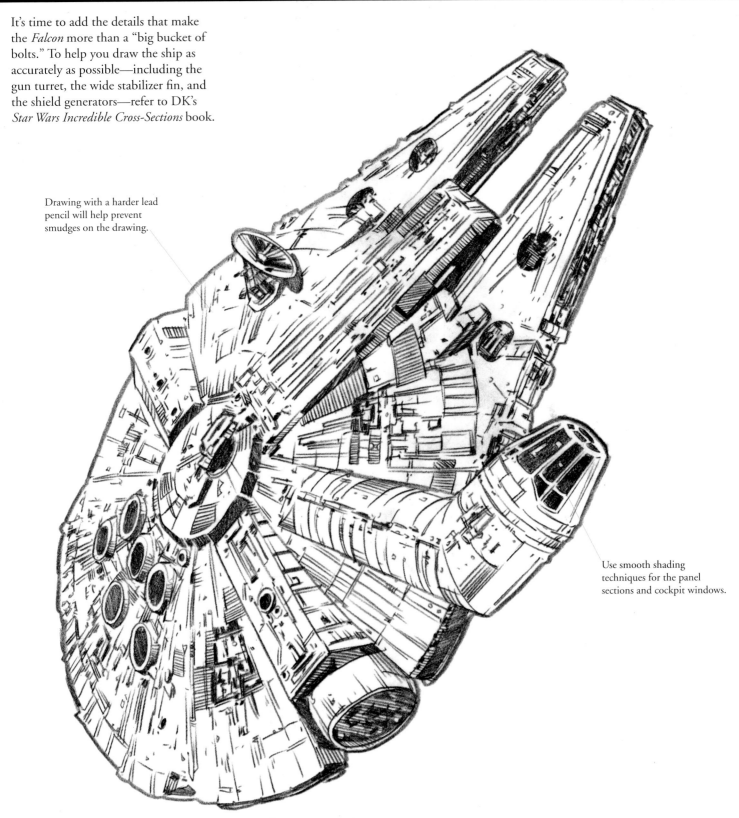

Use smooth shading techniques for the panel sections and cockpit windows.

BACKSEAT DRIVERS

The droids C-3PO and R2-D2 are frequent passengers onboard the *Millennium Falcon*. R2-D2 is an astromech droid, so his skills are useful to any pilot needing on-flight maintenance. But C-3PO's endless stream of statistics are not always so welcome, though the golden droid can sometimes prove useful—such as when he translates the language of the *Falcon*'s main computer, enabling Solo to fix the ship. Mostly, however, the droids stay in the background, where they amuse themselves by bickering with each other or playing hologames with Chewbacca.

A QUICK GETAWAY

With the *Falcon*'s handy hyperspace drive, the ship outruns a variety of worthy opponents from Star Destroyers to an unexpected space slug. With a Class 0.5 hyperdrive, it is nearly twice as fast as the fastest Imperial warships. However, when it runs into the Death Star, it cannot escape the powerful tractor beam that pulls it in. In the illustration on the right, the artist has angled the ship to indicate a sudden jump to hyperspace to escape the Imperial Star Destroyer.

FINAL INK DRAWING

Lightly ink the final illustration. Only use heavier ink applications to larger shaded areas such as the windows, vent holes, and outer edge of the ship. To give the ship a sense of motion, feel free to add speed lines at the rear of the ship.

Darken the outline of the ship and use lighter lines on the ship's hull to add depth.

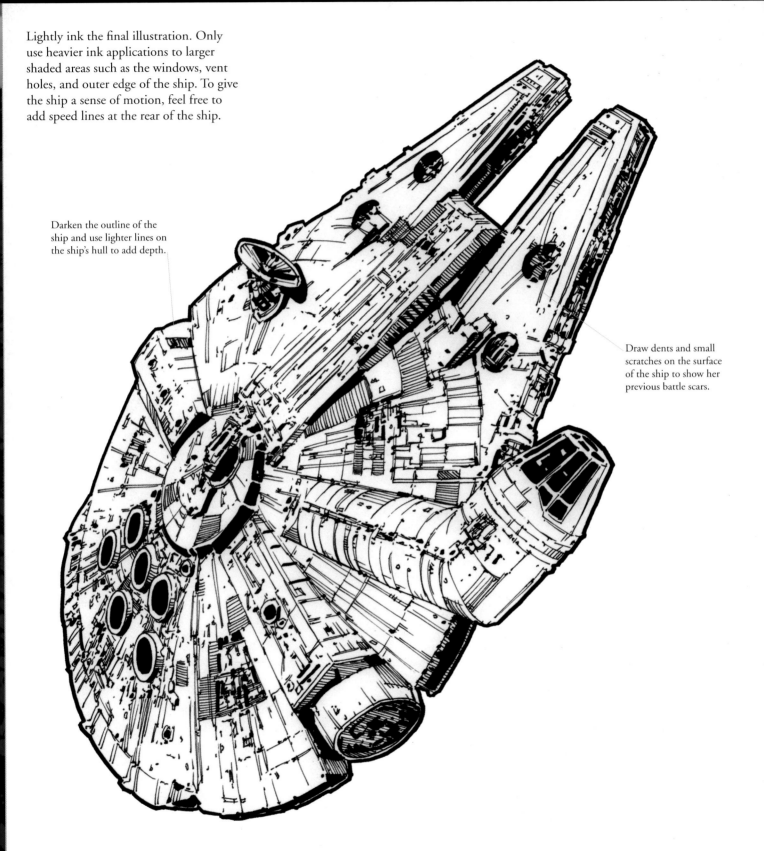

Draw dents and small scratches on the surface of the ship to show her previous battle scars.

INKING AND COLORING

Now that you have learned the basics of drawing—bring your pencil sketch to life by adding ink and color!

Inking an illustration emphasizes the power of a portrait's lines. The stark contrast between black and white adds drama and intensity to the subject of your drawing. The solid darkness of the ink gives the piece clean lines for a more polished look.

Applying color amplifies the mood of a character or scene. While certain color combinations make a character like Boba Fett pop off the page, other colors can express tense, calm, or melancholy moments.

The following pages explain the tools of the trade, as well as inking and coloring techniques that will teach you how to illustrate *Star Wars* like the pros.

So gather up your ink and colors and let's get started!

INK

INKING

Professional comic-book artists and illustrators finalize many of their pieces with ink for a more polished look. To darken lines, use pens, markers, and special brushes.

Dip pen ink

Ink for technical pen

Ink

Whether you want the blackest of India ink or the sateen finish of a shellac-based ink, an ink type exists for every preference. The best kind of ink doesn't clog and covers well. Experiment with various acrylic, drawing, calligraphy, and mixed media inks.

Dip pen and nibs

.25

Technical pen

Felt-tips and markers

These create thin or thick lines depending on their size and the pressure applied. Consider using fade-resistant, smudge-proof, archival-quality ink to preserve the quality of your drawing.

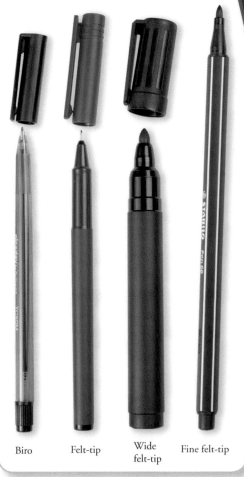

Different sizes of brushes

Brushes

The size and thickness of the brush often determines the width of a line. Try using a watercolor brush for making fine lines in your illustration. Practice with different bristle types.

Biro   Felt-tip   Wide felt-tip   Fine felt-tip

Dip pens

Dip pens have a removable pen point, which must be dipped in ink repeatedly to use, but its flexible tip allows for interesting variations in line widths.

Technical pens

Engineers and architects like to use technical pens for their consistent lines. The pens are refillable and come in various tip sizes.

Process white

Correction fluid

Correction tape

CORRECTION FLUID

Erasers won't make ink mistakes disappear, but white ink will! Plus, with a little practice, you can easily create your own galaxy of stars and distant planets in a black sky.

COLOR

COLORFUL CHARACTERS

Life should never be viewed in simple black or white, so why should your art? Adding color to an illustration can make an interesting alien pop off the page. Whether it's Yoda's green hue or Darth Vader's blazing red lightsaber, color can be applied in a number of ways.

Watercolors

Paint

For more fresh tones try using watercolors. For heavier and more opaque colors, try using gouache. Oil paints allow for easy mixing of colors but take longer to dry. Acrylics dry faster and can be mixed with water or used straight out of the tube for different looks. Experiment with non-traditional paints such as finger paints, food coloring, and fabric paint for different effects.

Oil

Acrylic

Gouache

Brushes

A classic artistic tool, brushes come in all kinds of styles, sizes, and bristles. With brushes an artist can create cool background effects and paint large spaces. Just remember to keep them clean and wash thoroughly after use.

Color pencils

Felt-tips and markers

Waterproof, permanent, and solvent-based markers deliver brilliant color in fine point or dense, broad strokes. To keep ink wet to mix on the page, use clear blending markers.

Fat marker

Color markers

Crayons and chalk

Softer than colored pencils, the rich colors of crayons cover large spaces and can be layered and scraped for additional effects. Chalk is easy to control and blend, and can cover large areas. Use it to create a soft-focus effect for your illustrations.

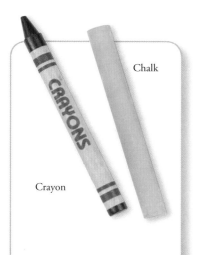

Chalk

Crayon

Color pencils

Less messy and more precise than most mediums, color pencils come in a cornucopia of colors. Best suited for fine sketching, pencils are also perfect for shading a drawing with precision.

Brushes

FROM PENCIL TO INK

FINISHING TOUCHES

Drawing with a pencil allows an artist to add fine lines and subtle shading. To give the piece a more polished look, however, inking is a necessity, even though some of the pencil details will disappear. Every artist has his or her own inking style, but certain techniques can be used to give the subject a distinct look.

Lightly sketch the outline of an Arakyd prowler 1000.

The medium inking highlights the tasking antenna.

The thermal detonator starts with a simple circle.

Start with basic rectangles and squares for the mouse droid.

The "Gonk" power droid begins life as two cubes with feet.

The inked lines add weight and dimension to the final illustration.

Instead of heavy pencil shading, finish with heavy inking near the body.

Begin with two spheres and a disc to create Rune Haako.

Now the basic shapes have become Rune Haako's data goggles and comlink.

VEHICLES: SLAVE I

Seismic Charge for Hire

Slave I started as an ordinary *Firespray*-class patrol craft used by police on the prison moon of Oovo 4. But once bounty hunter Jango Fett added his extensive modifications, it became one of the most highly-feared ships in the galaxy. Jango's son Boba Fett would later inherit the attack ship and use it to seek out the fugitive Han Solo for Jabba the Hutt.

YOUR TURN!

The best way to learn how to draw a vehicle is to sketch cars and trucks you see on the street. Notice how objects are reflected differently on hub-caps from how they are on the windshield. Hone your skills at drawing realistic-looking cars, trucks, vans, scooters, and motorcycles—it will come in handy when you are illustrating *Star Wars* spacecrafts and vehicles.

Draw the circular base to look like a satellite dish.

Erase your initial lines as the sketch progresses.

Slave I is at a 3/4 angle.

1) Sketch a rough outline of the ship's body. Draw both a vertical and horizontal line to keep the ship symmetrical.

2) Add more detail to the ship including the windshield, wings, and missile launcher.

Remember who and what lurks inside the ship's cockpit.

Show the reflection hitting the windshield.

3) Begin shading the other plating of the ship, as well as highlighting the finer features, such as the energy shield generator.

4) Ink the drawing to show the ship's distinct coloring, the direction of the light source, as well as its original Oovo security markings.

STEP-BY-STEP

MANGA STYLE

Manga, which literally means "playful images," represents a popular Japanese style of comics. Influenced by Disney during the 1940s and classic "ukiyo-e" paintings, Japanese artists created their own style by drawing cartoonish characters with exaggerated facial features. The style also includes unrealistic body proportions, big hair, and extreme emotions.

Star Wars was drawn in a manga style in this comic book series from 1998.

While some manga styles are overtly cutesy, other styles can be more realistic, as with this example of Luke Skywalker from *A New Hope*.

When drawing in a manga style, don't forget to follow the rules of perspective and foreshortening as you would in other sketches.

Light from Tatooine's two suns hits the scene from the front. Intensify the dark shadows behind Luke and his home.

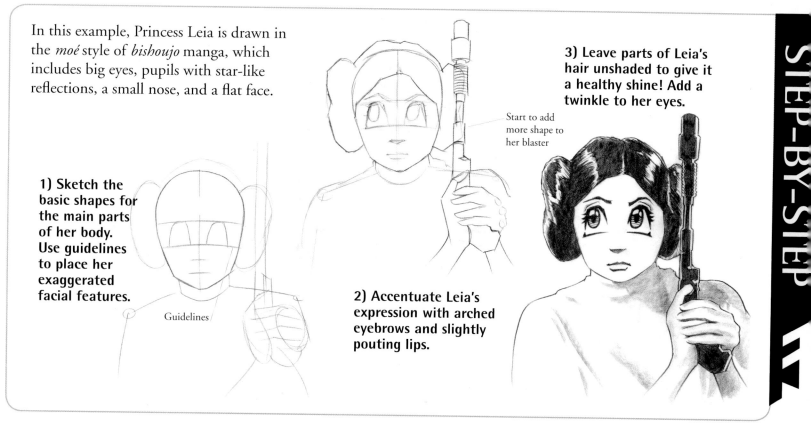

In this example, Princess Leia is drawn in the *moé* style of *bishoujo* manga, which includes big eyes, pupils with star-like reflections, a small nose, and a flat face.

1) Sketch the basic shapes for the main parts of her body. Use guidelines to place her exaggerated facial features.

Guidelines

2) Accentuate Leia's expression with arched eyebrows and slightly pouting lips.

Start to add more shape to her blaster

3) Leave parts of Leia's hair unshaded to give it a healthy shine! Add a twinkle to her eyes.

MANGA CHARACTERS

Princess Leia means business in this pose. Her large feet and hands give her an almost mecha (robotic) look.

While it's obvious Luke's feet and hands are also oversized, notice his tiny head, waist, thighs, and accessories.

The body language of this Rebel pilot conveys his attitude. Make sure you still use the basics of action sketching when working in a manga style.

COLOR BASICS

THE PROPERTIES OF COLOR

When you see color, it is really the reflection of light bouncing off of an object. A hue is a particular gradation of color. The lightness or darkness of a color is described as its value, while its intensity is measured by the amount of a color's purity and strength.

COLOR WHEEL

Artists use this wheel—divided into Primary, Secondary, and Tertiary categories—to show how mixing colors makes other colors. Yellow, blue, and red are primary colors. Secondary colors like orange, green, and purple are created by mixing two primary colors equally. Tertiary colors are a mix of a primary and a secondary color.

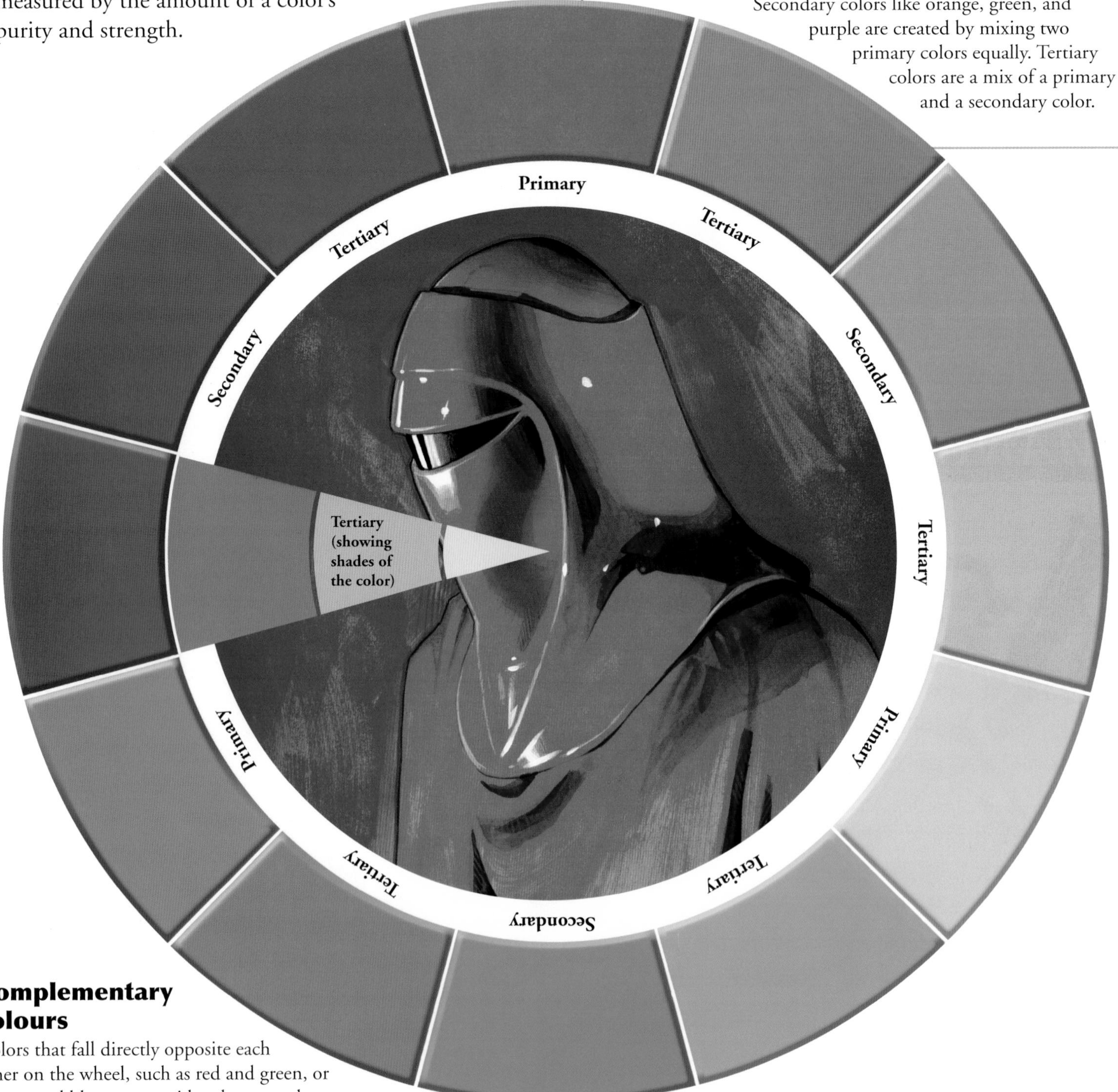

Primary

Tertiary

Tertiary

Secondary

Secondary

Tertiary

Primary

Tertiary

(showing shades of the color)

Primary

Primary

Tertiary

Tertiary

Secondary

Complementary colours

Colors that fall directly opposite each other on the wheel, such as red and green, or orange and blue, are considered to complement each other. These contrasting colors can add drama.

FIRE AND ICE

Practice using different color combinations to give a specific feel to an illustration. The hot tones of red, orange, and yellow reflect Princess Leia's intensity, while the cold hues of blue and white used for the stormtrooper mirror the austerity of the Empire.

COLOR MOODS

You can influence the mood of the scene just by using certain hues. Change the choice of color scheme to add atmosphere and emotion to an illustration.

Cold
Blues, purples, and whites are cold colors, which are calm and relaxing to the viewer.

Hot
Reds, yellows, and oranges infuse heat and passion into the drawing.

Moody
Many tertiary colors can add a somber or melancholy tone to an illustration.

YODA

As a short yet powerful Jedi Master, Yoda teaches patience and perseverance in his invaluable lessons. Using these two qualities, you can really bring your drawings of the little green Jedi to life. Aged around 900 years, Yoda's face is lined with experience and his eyes reflect all the knowledge of good and evil that he has seen in his lifetime.

EXPERT ADVICE

Every wrinkle on Yoda's face tells a story. Take care when illustrating his facial expressions. Study his portrayal in the films and comics. How do the differences in style best highlight his skill as a swordsman, or concern for his Padawans?

CHARACTER HISTORY

While much of Yoda's history is clouded in mystery, it is certain that his influence on his numerous Padawans through thoughtful lessons remains unparalleled. As a sage instructor at the Jedi Temple, Yoda councils the ways of the Force during battle. As a respected elder Jedi Master on the Council, Yoda advises Jedi Knights, as well as his Wookiee allies, during the Clone Wars, and continues to be invaluable while the unsavory plans of Emperor Palpatine reveal themselves.

SIZE MATTERS NOT

Standing at only 66 centimeters tall, Yoda might be small but his exceptional lightsaber skills and mastery of the Force make him a fierce warrior not to be underestimated. Acting as a general during the Clone Wars, he saw his fair share of battle. But he wasn't one to stand by the sidelines. Fighting against his former pupil Count Dooku in a fantastic display of lightsaber prowess and then later against Emperor Palpatine, Yoda's fighting and defensive skills are legendary. When you are drawing Yoda in combat mode, experiment with acrobatic poses, accentuating his small compact body and short limbs.

ROUGH PENCIL DRAWING

This illustration of Yoda draws attention to his three-fingered hands, which are often used to both fight with the Force as well as protect himself against the Emperor's destructive Force lightning. Sketch with loose, light lines and use basic shapes for Yoda's body.

This illustration of Yoda draws attention to his three-fingered hands, which are often used to both fight with the Force as well as protect himself against the Emperor's destructive Force lightning. Sketch with loose, light lines and use basic shapes for Yoda's body.

FINAL PENCIL DRAWING

Next, finalize the details in Yoda's body and clothing. As Yoda might advise—don't rush this process! Pay special attention to Yoda's eyes and the creases in his forehead to fully express his penetrating stare.

Add lines to further define Yoda's face and hands, as well as the wooden texture of his gimer stick.

Use crosshatching and smooth shading techniques to darken folds in Yoda's robe.

A MINUTE MENTOR

As a Master at the Jedi Temple, Yoda has instructed every youngling before they began their training apprenticeships with their assigned Masters. For 800 years, Yoda trained every notable Jedi except for Anakin Skywalker, which may explain his destined fall to the dark side. Years later, however, Luke Skywalker sought him out on the advice of Obi-Wan Kenobi, for much-needed teachings on the ways of the Force. In this illustration we see the stoic Yoda landing on the deserted planet of Dagobah after fleeing from the Emperor. Notice Yoda's proud but sad posture as he contemplates his future life on the uninhabited planet and the destruction of the Jedi order and democracy.

VISION QUEST

Initially Yoda is reluctant to train Luke during the latter's stay on Dagobah, as he shows signs of stubbornness and unwillingness to trust in the ways of the Force, much like his father, the doomed Anakin Skywalker. But Luke persists and, under Yoda's guidance, is able to become a Jedi. Being a Master of the Force, Yoda is very wise and perceptive of the world around him. Try to add this quality to your drawings of him.

INSPIRED BY GREATNESS

Originally drawn as a gnome-like creature, Yoda's form took more shape at the hands of make-up and creatures supervisor Stuart Freeborn, who modeled the elfin luminary's face on his own and partly on the face of Nobel Prize-winning theoretical physicist Albert Einstein. Notice in particular his ridged cranium, puckered mouth, and snubby nose, as well as the enlarged ears and green skin. His three-fingered hands and feet have long claws.

FINAL INK DRAWING

Now blacken the hidden space inside the robe as well as the costume's deep creases. Parallel lines and crosshatching add drama to the illustration. Erase all pencil lines after you have used them to guide you during the inking process.

Add loose, detached lines for Yoda's white hair.

Make Yoda's ears pointy, but not too rigid.

CREATING A COMIC

Open any comic book and you'll see exciting action shots, emotionally charged close-ups, and detailed backdrops—all used to tell a captivating story.

While it's up to the writer to create a script, it's the artist's responsibility to make the story come to life visually. Sometimes the writer and illustrator are the same person but most comics are created by a number of different individuals.

In the following pages, you'll read about all the ways to convey tension, suspense, and action in a story just by experimenting with different "camera" angles, layout designs, and speech balloons.

On the very last page, we've included stencils of speech balloons and explosions to help you complete your comic book page.

After reading this final chapter, you'll become a full-fledged creator of your own comic books.

SHOTS AND ANGLES

PENCIL, ANGLE, ACTION!

Comic books all start life as a script or a plot point, to entice the reader into turning page after page. A full script breaks down the story into comic panels and character dialog. The plot organizes the arrangement of incidents in a story, and carefully guides the development of the action. The comic book artist serves as the director, using camera angles that could include a wide shot of the background or a close-up of the hero.

EXPERT ADVICE

The next time you watch a movie count the number of establishing, medium, or close-up shots. Notice how a close-up shot can serve as a plot point, or even a clue in a mystery. Study how directors may use one type of shot more than other types.

ESTABLISHING SHOT

This is a wide shot that sets the scene. It often shows the background as well as the character. The size of the shot helps the reader understand the location and the emphasis is on the scene rather than a character.

MEDIUM SHOT

As the camera moves closer to Anakin more details in his appearance are visible, while the background begins to disappear. Even though a medium shot doesn't reveal a great deal about Anakin's facial expression, the body language remains obvious. This kind of shot helps move the story to the next crucial moment.

CLOSE-UP

This shot zooms in closer, tightly framing Anakin's face. A close-up like this exposes his emotion and true character, which is crucial for a reader to understand a panel's message without dialog. A close-up can also be used to introduce an important character in the story.

Keep things simple. Now that you can draw a multitude of characters, droids, and creatures, don't be tempted to use all of them in one scene. Clutter can distract the reader from the main point you are trying to make in a panel. Limit the extra content and you will keep the viewer focused on the primary message of the story.

Up shot

At ground level, the camera looks up toward Anakin. This adds the illusion of height to the character, making him seem powerful. The background element of the cliff side where Anakin stands also hints at his ominous demeanor.

Down shot

When the focus is on Anakin from above, he looks towards the camera with great interest. At this angle, he also appears almost vulnerable. A down shot used to establish a scene is referred to as an aerial shot.

Inset panel

To see the action unfold from two points of view, comic artists use inset panels. In this main panel the infamous face guard descends to take its place on Darth Vader's face, whereas the inset is a close-up of his eye revealing the horror of the situation.

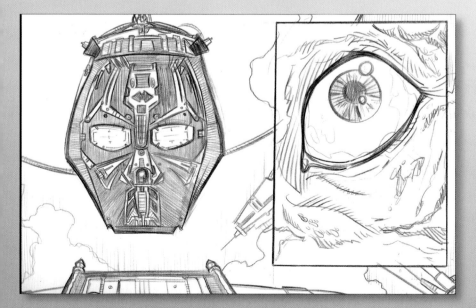

Composition

The specific arrangement of a character and the background elements behind him are important. The artist uses composition to direct a viewer's eye as he or she looks at the panel. The more an image is cropped, the less action the viewer sees.

THE SCRIPT

TAKE ONE

Much like a movie screenplay, a comic-book script describes the action in each panel of each page, including character dialog and captions.

Comments

Once an artist receives a script, it's up to him or her to bring those words to life with images. Read the following script example and visualize how you would storyboard the characters in action.

"CAP"

Short for "captions," which can represent the character's thoughts.

"OFF"

To signify that something is happening or that someone is present "off" the panel, where the viewer cannot see.

"SFX"

This is to signify that the word following is a sound effect.

JANGO FETT: SCUM AND VILLAINY #X
Script for 24 pages
Bonnie Writer (444)555-0000

Panel One
LONG SHOT. Day. The blistering streets of Mos Espa, Tatooine. We see various low-life species making their way here and there.
1 CAP: Yet another wretched hive of scum and villainy.
2 CAP: But Mos Espa isn't so bad.
3 CAP: It's practically a vacation spot for a bounty hunter like me.
4 CAP: I fit in here. It's my kind of people.
5 CAP: My kind of scum.

Panel Two
CLOSE SHOT. We see a female hand gripping a lightsaber in the foreground. In the background, we see Jango Fett marching intently down one of the vendor alleys.
6 CAP: Besides, no one would ever think to come looking for me in the Outer Rim.
7 CAP: Of course, even Mos Espa can be full of surprises.

Panel Three
Jango stops in his tracks as he hears a familiar voice from behind.
8 OFF: End of the line, Fett!
9 JANGO: You Jedi are becoming more and more irritating. I should have finished you with the rest of them on Kamino.

Panel Four
Behind Jango we see Rac, a young Jedi Knight who ignites her saber, ready for action.
9 RAC: Now your time has come, and you'll pay for what you've done.
10 SFX: VZZZZUMMM!

Panel Five
MEDIUM SHOT. Jango spins around in a dynamic stance, blasters in hand.
11 JANGO: It's true no one lives forever.
12 JANGO: But mark my words...
13 JANGO: ...I'll never die by the Jedi sword!

THUMBNAILS

Comic-book artists often draw small sketches of how a panel or comic book page should appear. These thumbnails help an artist experiment with composition, layout, and angles for the same scene without wasting time completing full pages to see how each end result will look.

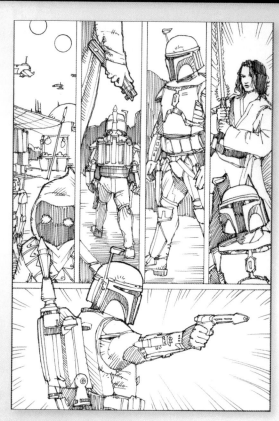

Layout Sample #1

To give a page a vertical feel, use long panels like this on the page. In this case, the vertical panels reveal the action that is about to take place, with the bottom panel acting as the most powerful moment on the page.

EXPERT ADVICE

Look at comics in your own collection to see how the story is revealed page by page. While some artists prefer to use the dramatic effect of vertical panels, others like to use a full page for one image to show multiple elements in an action scene. Practice different layouts for your own story to see which ones you like best.

Layout Sample #3

In this layout, the horizontal panel at the top helps set the scene, while the rest of the panels allow the reader to follow the main character as his duel is about to begin, giving the page a strong sense of rhythm.

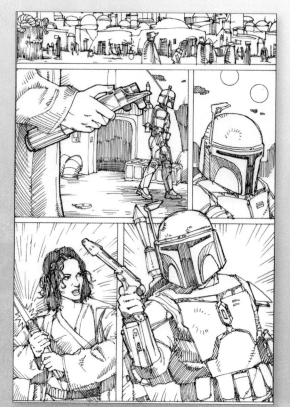

Layout Sample #2

The horizontal panel at the top is a wide, establishing shot while the others below—which utilize both medium and close-up shots—allow the reader a head-on view of the tension mounting between the two opponents.

FINAL LAYOUT

FETT ACCOMPLI

Using the last thumbnail layout from the previous page, you can see the step-by-step process of turning ideas into a final piece. By using pencil, marker pen, then ink, you can create a really professional comic-book page.

PUTTING IT TOGETHER

The final page looks intimidating until it's broken down step by step. Begin as always with the pencil sketch. As you draw the establishing shot as well as other panel components, include details like the ridges in the lightsaber hilt and the wrinkles in Boba's pants. This will make inking easier to tackle.

1
In the pencil drawing, X marks the spots where heavy inking should occur. Multiple lines and feathering are used in the shadows on buildings and creases in clothing to give them texture and realism.

2
With a marker pen, add depth to the illustrated panels by outlining specific characters you want the eye to focus on in each scene, like Boba Fett. Notice in the last panel how Boba literally looks like he's popping out of the panel and off the page.

HAW! GOTCHA, JEDI!

GOTCHA DEAD TO---

SLIIINNNNN!

WORDS AND SOUNDS

When a character speaks aloud or thinks, the words are shown in word balloons or thought bubbles. Jagged balloon lines and unique lettering represent sound effects, while dotted lines imply whispering. Boxes found on the edges of the panels contain the voice of the narrator.

3

To create the final piece, use the marker layout as a guide. If you have a light-table, put your page over the marker layout so that you can keep the correct layout and proportions. The spaces of heavy inking add weight to the illustration. Background lines are added behind Boba to give him more presence in the panel. Now this looks like a comic book page!

INDEX

ACKNOWLEDGMENTS

Tom Hodges: I would like to thank my Mom and Dad, Steve and Joyce Hodges, and my siblings Steve, Michele, Brian, and Sean for their support. Paul Federico, Paul Slack, and Pat Miggin for getting a guy's back. And last but not least, my loving wife, Terri, and my son, Logan, for all of their patience and support.

Matt Busch: I would like to thank all the friends, family, and fans that have supported my artistic endeavors over the years. I would also like to thank Rachel Rossilli, Nick Forshee, and Nicole Minaudo for their volunteer work, modeling as various characters in this book.

Bonnie Burton: After my first glance of an AT-AT trudging through the snowy battlefield, my notebooks were soon covered with nothing but *Star Wars* doodles thanks to the imagination of George Lucas and his crew of gifted artists. I also thank Amy Gary and Jonathan Rinzler at LucasBooks for the chance to make such a cool book. Special thanks goes to my dad who introduced me to the "happy little trees" painter Bob Ross, and to my mom for buying me endless tubes of finger paints to cover canvases and my little brother.
In addition to this book's talented illustrators—Matt Busch and Tom Hodges—a huge thanks goes to the other artists who offer their handy tips on the Learn to Draw tutorials on http://www.starwars.com/kids.

DK would like to thank Siu Chan for additional DTP work, Jon Hall for the color wheel, Amy Junor and Laura Gilbert for editorial assistance; Lance Kreiter and Riko Frohnmayer from Dark Horse comics for their assistance with sourcing comic book images on pages: 14 (r), 17 (br), 30 (t, l), 33 (tl), 36 (tl), 38 (tr, ml, b), 40, 50 (ml), 56 (bl), 58, 78 (tr), 82 (mr, br), 84, 86–87, 92 (bl). DK would also like to thank the following creative talents for their contributions to this book: Brad Anderson, Christopher Chuckry, Steve Crespo, Digital Chameleon, Dave Dorman, Jan Duursema, Martin Egeland, Davidé Fabbri, George Freeman, Henry Gilroy, Heroic Age, Hoon, Chris Horn, Jason Hvam, Dan Jackson, Rafael Kayan, Ken Kelly, Ray Kryssing, Miles Lane, Darko Macan, Harold MacKinnon, Ron Marz, Dave McCaig, Ted Naifeh, David Nestelle, John Ostrander, Kilian Plunkett, P. Craig Russell, Mark Schultz, Galen Showman, Howard Shum, Lisa Stamp, Dave Stewart, Hisao Tamaki, Robert Teranishi, Tim Truman, Christian dalla Vecchia, Francisco Ruis Velasco, Adam Warren, Doug Wheatley, Ryder Windham.

Tom Hodges created artwork on pages: 42–43, 57, 59 and trace overlay, 78 (b, bl, ml), 79 (top row), 88–89.

Matt Busch created artwork on pages: 1, 3, 4–5, 6–7, 8–9, 10, 12 (bottom row), 13, 14 (l, ml), 15, 16, 17 (l, tr), 18–19, 20–21, 22–23, 24–25, 26–27, 28, 29, 30 (mb, br), 31, 32, 33 (tr, mb), 34–35, 36 (b, r), 37, 38 (tl), 39, 41 and trace overlay, 44–45, 46–47, 48–49, 50 (tr and bottom row), 51, 52–53, 54-55, 56 (t, r), 60–61, 62–63, 64–65, 66–67, 68–69, 70–71 and trace overlay, 72–73, 76–77, 80–81, 82 (bl), 83, 85 and trace overlay, 91, 92 (t, mr), 93, 96.

m=middle b=bottom t=top l=left r=right

Tom Hodges has fast become a fan favorite within the *Star Wars* Universe. Recently named one of wizarduniverse.com's "Top 5 to Watch in 2006," his work appears on the very popular starwars.com Hyperspace webstrip series. **www.tomhodges.com**

Matt Busch has been regarded as one of the top "entertainment illustrators" of today and his work can be regularly seen in official *Star Wars* projects. He currently professes in the Media & Communication Arts at Macomb Community College. **www.mattbusch.com**

Bonnie Burton is a prolific writer, particularly on all things *Star Wars*. As an Online Content Developer at Lucasfilm, she has written a multitude of step-by-step drawing tutorials. Her first book: *Never Threaten to Eat Your Co-Workers: Best of Blogs* is out now. **www. grrl.com**